WHEN THE GOING GETS TOUGH...

Yisroel Roll

LEVIATHAN PRESS
BOOKS THAT MAKE A DIFFERENCE

When The Going Gets Tough
by Yisroel Roll

Leviathan Press
17 Warren Road Suite 19
Baltimore, Maryland 21208
(410) 653-0300

ISBN 1-881927-26-1

Cover illustration by Julius Ciss (410) 784-1416 www.juliusciss.com
Cover design by Staiman Design
Page layout by Zisi Berkowitz

Distributed to the trade by NBN (800) 462-6420
Distributed to Judaica booksellers by
The Judaica Press, Inc.
718-972-6200   800-972-6201
info@judaicapress.com
www.judaicapress.com

All books from Leviathan Press are available at bulk order discounts
for educational, promotional and fundraising purposes.
For information call (800) 538-4284.

Manufactured in the United States of America

This book is
dedicated in memory of

Rosa Selig, z"l

רייזל בת יעקב, ז"ל

❧ ❧ ❧

She opens her mouth with wisdom;
and the law of kindness
is on her tongue.

Proverbs 31:26

❧ ❧ ❧

Warmly dedicated by her grandson,

**Jonathan Symons,
London, England**

TABLE OF CONTENTS

ACKNOWLEDGEMENTS

SOME MAY FEEL THAT GRATITUDE IS difficult to express. It may make us feel vulnerable, weak and dependent. I find it liberating. In my travels I have met wonderfully insightful and supportive people with whom I have connected and have interwoven thoughts, vision and dreams. I express my sincere thanks and appreciation to the following individuals who have shared and supported my dreams and programs over the years, and who have encouraged the development of this project:

Jonathan Symons, London

Bernard Siegel, Baltimore

Hannah Storch, Baltimore

Frank and Danielle Sarah Storch, Baltimore

The late Sir Emmanuel Kaye, z"l, and Lady Elizabeth Kaye, London

Dr. Michael and Penny Sinclair, London

Dr. Leon and Janice Bernstein, London

Sol and Jill Potel, London

Anthony and Claudia Goldstein, London

Michael and Natalie Cutler, London

Gary and Ellen Davis, Greenwich, Connecticut

Shlomie and Breindy Ehrentreu, Toronto

Dr. Yisroel and Robbin Ingber, Toronto

Gary and Malkie Torgow, Detroit

I would also like to express my sincere gratitude to the following individuals:

Rabbi Professor David Gottlieb, of Jerusalem, for his review of the manuscript, his insights and encouragement.

Rabbi Akiva and Leah Mann, of Boca Raton, Florida, for their wisdom, guidance and friendship.

Rabbi Shimon and Miriam Apisdorf for believing in this project.

The team at Judaica Press/Leviathan Press: Aryeh Mezei for his professionalism and guidance; Nachum Shapiro for his creativity, insights and vision; and Rena Joseph and Bonnie Goldman for their work at editing and enhancing the manuscript.

Hadassah Webster Diamant, of London, for her guidance and inspiration.

Finally, I would like to thank our children Rivka, Dovid Simcha, Rina, Yehudah and Channah for deeply enriching our lives.

FOREWORD

by Dr. Abraham Twerski, M.D.

YES, THERE ARE PROBLEMS IN LIFE. Experience has shown that neither geographic changes nor tranquilizers solve anything. These are nothing but escapist maneuvers.

But why escape? True, if one is inside a building that is ablaze, one escapes. However, if something is smoldering in a wastebasket, one does not flee the building. Rather, one takes a cup of water and extinguishes the flame. Why the difference? Because the challenge of a burning building is overwhelming, far beyond one's coping skills. The smoldering wastebasket, on the other hand, is well within one's capacity.

Many people use a variety of maneuvers to escape from problems that are well within their coping capacity. If people would only be more aware of their strengths and their ability to cope with life situations rather than flee from them, they could avoid the distress of unresolved problems that escalate and become more complicated.

In *When the Going Gets Tough*, Rabbi Roll provides us with valuable techniques for coping. I feel a kinship with Rabbi Roll, having written two books on, "It's Not as Tough as You Think". This is an anecdotal approach that may help minimize the apparent magnitude of problems. Rabbi Roll complements this by showing us ways in which we can utilize our inner strengths to cope effectively with whatever tough spots do exist.

There was a story in the newspaper about a woman in Ohio, whose eighteen-month-old child got away from her and crawled underneath a parked car. The mother panicked, ran over, lifted the car and grabbed her baby. Four strong men could probably not have lifted the car. Where did this 110 pound woman get such superhuman strength?

A similar example is of a patient, in a manic phase of his illness, who shoveled snow for forty-eight consecutive hours! This would have killed anyone else. Where does such extraordinary strength come from?

The answer is that we all have sources of strength within us to which we usually do not have access and which only emerge under extreme circumstances. This is true psychologically as well as physically. If we could only tap into our hidden resources, we could achieve much greater things in life.

Rabbi Roll provides his wisdom in a very palatable vehicle, helping us reach into our inner selves to reveal our untapped potential.

For Julie
"As the rose among the thorns,
so is my love among the daughters" (Song of Songs 2:2).

INTRODUCTION

LIFE IS PERSONAL. The way you live your life depends upon your attitude toward life's journey—it's all about how you personally think and react. Your life's direction is up to you—so let this book be your guide to self-discovery. Try, if you will, to read this book as an internal dialogue. Play out these ideas in your mind, and let yourself feel and experience them, so you can learn to get good at the art of living. Use this book as your personal handbook to start getting a handle on your inner "self."

I approach each issue in this book from two dimensions—the spiritual and the mystical. The spiritual perspective asks you to deal with the issue from the perspective of your spiritual center. But what is your spiritual center? The human being is a composite creature comprised of a body plus "something else." That "something else" is your spiritual dimension. It is that which animals don't have and which make you uniquely human. For example, human beings can learn from the mistakes of past generations—animals cannot. People can reflect on the goal and purpose of life—animals cannot. People can think about what they must do to become better people. I doubt that animals consciously think about self-improvement. Human beings can delay gratification of physical drives for moral and ethical reasons—animals cannot. Except for the maternal instinct, animals in the wild probably do not sacrifice of their comfort and possessions in order to help a strange animal. People can be altruistic.

The aggregate of all the unique features of a human being that distinguishes us from animals is what we call the "spirit." That part of your psyche that is the choosing center, whereby you initiate choices to activate your spiritual self, is called your spiritual center. Acting spiritually then, means you are striving to develop yourself into the best human being you can be. This book can serve as your guide to achieve that, when the going gets tough.

Judaism informs us that there is an even deeper level underlying your spirituality. That is your mystical self. Think about that wonderful London landmark of Big Ben, the famous clock tower near Westminster Abbey. The face of the clock can be compared to your spiritual self. It has a beautiful face and adorns London's skyline. But behind the face of Big Ben are an intricate series of hidden gears, pulleys and mechanisms that make Big Ben tick. Without these highly tuned and finely-engineered systems, Big Ben wouldn't work. The gears are the hidden components of Big Ben's makeup, which explain the real story behind Big Ben and which drive it forward in time.

This can be compared to your mystical dimension. It is intimately connected with your spiritual center, but it is the gear mechanism that drives your spirituality. Therefore, after we look at each issue from the spiritual perspective, we will go behind the spiritual face and take a look at the issue from its mystical root— or source. When you see, no when you feel, the issue reaching its source, then let it penetrate your soul. That is the dimension which is at the core and which drives your spiritual center.

WHEN THE GOING GETS TOUGH...

A SPIRITUAL PERSPECTIVE

WHEN THE GOING GETS TOUGH... the tough do not get going. And they certainly don't go shopping.

They don't?

No.

Then what do they do?

They get... thinking.

So when I lose my job, my marriage is on the rocks, my kids are on drugs and I am two months behind on my mortgage or rent payments, I am not supposed to "get going" and push myself to solve my problems?

Right.

Just "think"?

Uh-huh.

And that's supposed to help?

It's the first step.

How, exactly?

When I am faced with a crisis, the first thing I need to address is my "thinking" or "mindset." If I see the issue before me as a crisis or problem, then I have adopted an adversarial or "fighting" attitude towards it. A more productive attitude is to view the crisis as a challenge or puzzle to solve, or, if not to solve, at least to deal with. It is not there to "break" me, but to bring out some hidden strength or ability from within me. It doesn't make me evil or bad or a loser. These difficulties are not sent only to me. Everyone faces difficulties in life. If I am willing to adopt this attitude, then I can "make friends" with the challenge, and then I am much better equipped to deal with it.

Isn't that just a mind game? By calling something a challenge instead of a problem, aren't I just fooling myself?

Not really. By abandoning the attitude that the world is out to get me, I transform debilitating negative energy into positive practical energy, which I can then use to help me solve my problem. My challenge is to harness as much of the mental and emotional energy at my disposal and make it work for me, instead of letting my pent-up anger and negativity drain me. This "mind game" has very real effects. Look at it this way—it takes thirty-eight facial muscles to frown, and only eighteen facial muscles to smile, so it makes sense to save my physical and emotional energy, and smile at my problem.

But, why me? Always me! Why does everyone else have it so easy?

First of all, it's not true. Even though it may appear that everything goes smoothly for my neighbor, friend, or boss, it is simply not true. That person may not be going through what I am, but each person faces challenges tailor made for him or her to bring out their unique hidden strengths and abilities. Each person has a unique array of inherited DNA, genes and chromosomes and a special set of parental, social and economic circumstances that make up his or her personality. Just as there are approximately six billion different human faces in the world, so too there are six billion different, special and unique individuals in the world, each with his or her own challenge. I am unique in the universe. No one else has my set of abilities and weaknesses, therefore no one else has my set of personal challenges.

Now, when a difficulty or problem comes my way, I must realize that it has never been presented to a person with my genetic or behavioral makeup ever before in world history. This is my special project or mission, for better or worse. It has my name on it. Only I can solve it or deal with it, in accordance with my unique set of abilities and weaknesses. My neighbor's marriage, job, house, and all of his or her issues are his to deal with. Looking over my shoulder or envying the situation of my neighbor is merely a waste of personal energy that I should be conserving to deal with my own challenges.

Now, when the "going gets tough," I consciously step into my "thinking mode" and view the difficulty as my unique challenge. I will be able to factor out any "why me?" issues and be able to focus on the task at hand of dealing with my challenge. I will not waste physical or emotional energy by comparing myself to others, but I will harness all of my special strengths and abilities to enable me to concentrate and deal with the issues before me. Therefore, when the going gets tough… the tough get *thinking*, and step into the positive mindset that is best suited to help meet the challenge before them.

A MYSTICAL PERSPECTIVE

LET'S COME CLEAN. God Himself has sent you the challenge you are currently facing. God has put you into the universe at this particular time, in this place, and with a certain set of strengths and weaknesses, in order to invite you to make your unique contribution to the world—to, in fact, change and uplift the world. God personally engineers events and customizes challenges just for you, so that you can develop your personality and actualize your potential by facing, dealing with, and growing through the ordeal. The going does get tough, because God is sending you challenges, in order to have you focus on the issue at hand, in order to help you develop your personality through dealing with the issue, and become a better person in the process.

Let's go deeper. "God" is really only one of the names of God. God's "real" name is *Ein Sof*, which means Never Ending, or Infinite One, or Perfect One. He sometimes chooses to relate to us with His attribute of Mercy. When He reveals His merciful side to us, we know Him—at that moment—as *Harachaman*, the Merciful One. But sometimes the *Ein Sof* relates to us with ordeals and challenges. Then He is known to us by His attribute of Justice—as the True Judge. And sometimes the *Ein Sof* treats us as a guiding parent, and is known to us as our "Father."

All of these "names" are merely terms of reference for us to be able to better understand the nature of our relationship with the *Ein Sof* at a particular point in time. The common denominator of all of these names is that the *Ein Sof* is never ending, unfolding and expansive. This does not mean that God is growing; it means that there is no limit to His growth.

The purpose of life—and you heard it here first—is to become as close to the Infinite One as is humanly possible. In order for us to come close, in fact to actually become like the *Ein Sof* we have to expand, unfold, and grow in our personalities, values, knowledge and character. For us to achieve this, the *Ein Sof* of necessity must challenge us with issues, ordeals, crises and problems, so that we can work through these issues, and grow and develop our character and horizons. Therefore, issues, ordeals, and crises are an essential part of the process of becoming the person you are supposed to become.

When God created man, He said, "Let us make man." Who was the "us" in that statement? The traditional answer is that God used characteristics of the animal world with which to create man. He used the majesty of the lion, the tenacity of the tiger and the resourcefulness of the fox. He "borrowed" these traits from "us"—the created animal kingdom—and incorporated them in the makeup and composition of the human persona. Hence, God consulted with "us," His "underlings," His creations, in order to fashion the human psyche.

There is a second, and more instructive answer to this question: Does God have a partner in the creation of man? Actually, yes. The partner is man himself. God is saying to man: Let us, you and I, together, create man. Let you and I together contribute to the creation, the "becoming" of man. Everything that God sends your way is designed to help you create and recreate yourself on a daily, ongoing, basis.

When the *Ein Sof* sends you a challenge, the basic question you must answer is the question implied within the challenge itself: What do you want from me, *Ein Sof*? What are you trying to teach me with this challenge? How can I become a better person through dealing with the issues that You, *Ein Sof*, are presenting to me? A challenge is the *Ein Sof*'s way of tapping you on the shoulder and saying: expand, grow and achieve your potential. Become like Me.

Hold it. What if I don't believe in the *Ein Sof*, God, the Creator, the Force or Something Up There?

Let's analyze this for a moment. There are many things in life that we can experience, even though we don't see them. Electricity, radio waves and gravity, for example. These are all invisible forces that exert power in the world. They cannot be seen, but they can be felt, or experienced.

You can also experience the *Ein Sof*, by becoming aware of the *Ein Sof* quality *within* you, that which is "Godly" in you. We call this a soul. The *Ein Sof* plants a unique spark of His essence in you, called the *chelek Eloka mima'al*, in order for you to be able to relate to Him.

Your soul is personal and unique, unlike any other. Whenever you experience a surge of meaning within your being, whenever you feel that there is something more to life than what you see—that is the movement of the *Ein Sof* within you. When, for example, you feel the sunset speaking to you, that is the soul within you being activated. If you feel the mountain air give you renewed energy as you view a waterfall from a mountain ridge, you are experiencing the Infiniteness outside of you and within you.

The *Ein Sof* is in everything and, at the same time, transcends everything. It is that which sustains the molecular structure of the universe—it is intimately connected with the world and everything in it. At the same time, it is the source of all that it is within the natural world—it is transcendent. The *Ein Sof* is imminent and transcendent at the same time. That is why we can feel close to God and simultaneously feel He is unknowable.

Not only is the *Ein Sof* the Creator of this amazing universe, He is also the Parent, Guide, and Supervisor of the world and everything in it. The Creator aspect of *Ein Sof* did not create the world, give it a spin and then go off for a holiday on one of His sandy white beaches in the Mediterranean. The *Ein Sof* is involved in guiding each and every individual in His world toward their own destinies, toward fulfilling their potential. He is a personal God. He is your personal God. It is through the challenges and issues that God presents us that He engages in a personal relationship with each of us. It is to the *Ein Sof*, the Source of your life energy, that you are challenged to direct your dialogue, yearnings, and prayers.

MY SECRET
WEAPON—THE
POWER OF CHOICE

A SPIRITUAL PERSPECTIVE

HOW DO I KNOW THAT I HAVE the ability and strength to solve, or at least deal with, my unique challenges? The simple truth is because I have a secret weapon that even *I* may not be aware that I possess.

Let me share with you how I discovered my secret weapon:

I woke up one morning and dragged myself to the bathroom. I looked in the mirror and was startled to find someone looking back at me. Even more astonishingly, it began to talk.

It said, "Who are you?"

"Yisroel Roll," I answered.

The image said, "I didn't ask you your name. I asked, 'Who are you?'"

I responded, "I am a rabbi."

The image said, "I didn't ask you what you *did* for a living. I asked, 'Who are you?'"

I tried again, "I am the husband of Julie, and father of…"

It said, "I didn't ask what your *relationships* were. I asked, 'Who are you?'"

Persevering, I ventured, "I have a home, I drive a…"

The image cut me off. "I didn't ask what you *owned*. I asked, 'Who are you?'"

Exasperated, I responded, "I give up. Who am I?"

It said, "You are a horse."

I replied indignantly, "A horse! What in the world do you mean?"

He explained, "Horses like to graze on the meadow. And I happen to know that you like to graze over a well-done rib steak with Southern barbecue sauce." (My wife is from the Deep South).

I said, "That's a pretty broad comparison. You'll have to do better than that."

He boldly replied, "When horses run in the meadow, there is always one horse who tries to run ahead of the pack. In your career, you always try to come up with new ideas and programs so that you too can run ahead of the competition. So, you are just like a horse."

Getting a little nervous, I stuttered, "Not bad. What else have you got?"

He said, "When a filly enters the meadow, the stallions get up on their hind legs and begin to neigh. It's their way of reacting to the filly. I happen to know that, when a woman enters the room while you are teaching a class, you subconsciously react by fixing your tie. You are a horse."

After having been compared not too inaccurately to a horse, I defiantly said, "Just a minute. I may have certain basic qualities similar in nature to a horse, but I am *not* a horse. I am the *rider* of the horse. I can direct and determine what I eat, what career I pursue, and my demeanor, and I can control my inner passions and desires. I can direct my 'horse-like' tendencies and guide them. I can raise myself above the level of the horse within me by reminding myself it is I who is in the saddle. So I can direct myself to meaningful activities because I am in control of the reins."

This odd encounter at the bathroom mirror was a revelation. I understood clearly who I was and that the horse within me is only Level One of my psyche—the animal-like part of my being. It is true that, like a horse, I have instincts, lusts, and passions that drive me. I have to admit that those impulses for self-preservation (i.e., food), self-gratification (i.e., pleasure), and power (i.e., money), rage so powerfully within me that I am sometimes convinced that these drives make up the sum total of my being. But that is not all I am. A rider within me directs these passions and animal instincts, the core of my real self—the part of me that decides which passions to pursue, which to delay pursuing, and which not to pursue at all.

The rider within me allows me to discern between worthwhile and meaningless activities. It allows me to appreciate sensations like beauty, symmetry and harmony. It allows me to "choose" to pursue spiritual endeavors like kindness, empathy and fairness. It inspires me to pursue values like truth, honesty and loyalty. It allows me to look inward and to become aware of my "self."

This core, this rider within me, is my spiritual center. It is the source of my decision-making process. It is the life energy which activates and motivates me. This is the source from which I can draw my hidden strength in order to help me deal with and meet life's challenges. The ability to access and activate my spiritual center is my secret weapon.

If I stop running through life in the "fast lane" and take a moment to reflect upon my character, I will be able to get in touch with my spiritual center. By so doing I will be able to get to know more of my authentic self. What a wonderful self-empowering feeling to be able to perform a quick "quality control" check on myself to ensure that I am channeling my drives and passions in the direction that I—meaning my spiritual center—want them to go, rather than allowing my passions to drive me.

My spiritual center enables me to summon all of the strengths, passions and drives within me to deal with a challenge from a position of conscious choice rather than with my usual knee-jerk instinctive reactions. My spiritual center—as my decision-making headquarters—ultimately gives me the strongest resource at my disposal—it provides the power and strength for me to choose how to deal with a challenge from a considered vantage point. And I can activate this secret weapon at will, any time I choose.

A MYSTICAL PERSPECTIVE

God created us as a combination of horse and rider. He gave us horse-like tendencies, such as eating, running ahead of the pack and reacting to the opposite sex. The horse-like part of us— the body—is the source of our physical drives, passions and lusts. However, as I've outlined, He also created a spiritual dimension in us, a rider for the horse—a soul.

If I freeze-dried my body and placed its components into a test tube, it would contain about seventy percent water, along with potassium, calcium, carbon, riboflavin and other essential ingredients necessary to "start your day the breakfast way."

If I sold my chemical elements to a pharmacist, "I" would probably be worth about one dollar and ninety-nine cents. My mother, however, thinks I am… priceless. Be that as it may, if all that I "am" is a certain selection of elements from the Periodic Table, then why is it that the freeze-dried test tube version of "me" doesn't do what I can do? The test tube components of me don't act motivated, enthused, inspired, moved, or sad. They just sit there. What's missing? The life force. The soul. This life energy is a spark of God Himself, which He invests and implants into every human being. It is this Godliness within us that gives each of us intrinsic value and worth. This is why Adam was created as a single being, to show that each human being has individual and intrinsic value as a unique creation of God Himself.

The soul is God's ambassador. When I listen to my soul's yearnings and I nourish them, then I am relating to the Godliness within me. I am developing my spirituality. I cannot nourish my soul with the same things that my body may crave. A new car, a steak or a beautifully remodeled kitchen will not do anything to satisfy my soul.

A story is told of the king's daughter who fell in love with a peasant farmer. They got married and he tried to provide for her needs. He brought her the things that made him happy—fine stalks of wheat, a beautifully dried out salami and some fresh fish. But no matter how hard he tried to please her, she was never satisfied, because she was used to the finer things in life.

The king's daughter represents the soul and the peasant farmer is the body. The body tries to satisfy the soul by bringing it physical pleasures. But the soul is not rooted in the physical world but in the spiritual world. The soul therefore craves spiritual satisfaction. It wants to be nourished by things like honesty, kindness, wisdom and truth.

If earthly pleasures are all we know, though, how can we ever hope to satisfy our souls? The answer is that lust, passion and a kosher hot dog at the ball game are not the only pleasures we know. There are deeper, more meaningful and more lasting pleasures—spiritual "delights" that are even better than a cold beer on a hot day. It may be hard to believe but its true.

The first thing we need to realize is that there are two ways in which the soul reacts, the pure decision-making part of the soul and the part of the soul which acts in response to our challenges. At the soul's core is the decision-making center of my being. I can decide to act instinctively or impulsively, or I can look at a given situation and choose to react spiritually. The act of deciding between right and wrong, between spiritual and physical paths, is the soul's domain.

The decision-making part of my soul—although given by God—is not controlled by God. God has given us free will or free choice to develop ourselves in the way that we see fit. If we choose to live our lives satisfying only our physical lusts, or if we choose to act destructively or to cause others pain, then God will *not* intervene because this would mean we do not have free will. We would be preprogrammed robots. God wants us to make freely-chosen moral choices, since it is only through exercising our free will that our souls can grow and achieve their potential.

Another aspect of exercising free will is how we react to the challenges that God sends our way. We can choose to be angry with God for giving us a rough ride and expend our energy being depressed and frustrated. Alternately, we can choose to delve into our souls and ask ourselves, what does God want us to learn from this situation? We can thus choose to exercise our free will positively, by working through the issues God is presenting us, and grow through the experience. We must realize, though, that God does not benefit from our choosing the spiritual pathway. We do. We get an opportunity to grow in personality and character. So when the going gets tough, the tough get *growing*.

If God preprogrammed me to act as He wanted, the world might be a nice place, but it would be a preprogrammed "God-made" world, which would have nothing to do with you or me. But that is not the purpose of the world. God created the world so that you and I could *choose* to make it a decent place out of our own free will and thereby earn our rewards. This world is for choosing between good and evil, and the world after this one— the World to Come—is for receiving reward for the choices we have made. Of course, we may get certain physical rewards in this world as God's investment in us, to allow us to continue to choose correctly in the spiritual aspects of our lives. But the ultimate reward for our spiritual choices will be in the World to Come, which is also a world of body and soul, albeit on a much higher level than the current world. As Rabbi Moshe Chaim Luzzato* states, "...in the renewed world, man will enjoy his reward with body and soul" (*Derech Hashem* 1:3:10).

Where on earth, then, is this "World to Come"? In one sense,

---

* A renowned Jewish mystic of the 18th century, also known as Ramchal.

it is *right here*. When we perform positive acts of kindness, or make other spiritual choices, we create a positive spiritual energy. This spiritual energy accumulates in the spiritual dimension that co-exists with this world. This spiritual energy *is* my World to Come. When I transition from this world of trial and travail into the next world, I will be able to access and I will live in this spiritual energy. It is in the next world that I will awaken to full consciousness and enjoy the 3D IMAX surround sound movie that is my life.

3

SPIRITUALITY

A SPIRITUAL PERSPECTIVE

GIVE ME A BREAK! What's all this talk about "spirituality," this "inner core" stuff? Life is about enjoying yourself! Ask anyone and they'll tell you that the purpose of life is just to "be happy." That means good food, good company, lots of money and in-laws who live out of town. That's the stuff that life is made of! You can't sell me that introspection and spirituality stuff. Get a life!

If life is just "eat, drink and be merry," then I am out of touch with reality. After all, the 1960s were the rebellion generation. The '70s were the "me" generation. The '80s were the junk bond, greed generation. The '90s were the "values" generation.

The new millennium, though, is the "get my act together" generation. I have a modicum of financial security, my own web page, and an annoying cell phone that plays Mozart. I may have a couple of kids, a house in the suburbs, and a cottage in the country. So what else is there?

What is missing is a sense of inner peace and fulfillment that I have not yet attained, a sense of meaning in life that has thus far eluded me. And the search for meaning is our most essential drive. I can begin to achieve it, however, by accessing my spiritual center.

Corporations are realizing that a more holistically balanced employee will be more productive and less likely to be head hunted. Increasingly, the phenomenon of corporate "downshifting" has been gaining ground. For example, a boss may send an employee home at six o'clock to have dinner with his family instead of keeping him working overtime. While some would argue that this is merely a function of the pursuit of greater profitability, others suggest that it is evidence of the "kinder, gentler nation" referred to by former United States President George Bush (the father, not the son). That is why more and more people are interested in attending weekend "self-improvement" seminars, something many would never have contemplated ten years ago, and why this generation is starting to spend more "quality time" with their families and investing more time and effort in making their relationships work.

In the post-9/11 world, people are focusing more on spirituality. We begin to realize that there must be a balance between the pursuit of personal happiness through self-gratification on the one hand, and a sense of true fulfillment on the other hand. Happiness is not as much a goal in itself as a by-product of living spiritually. By dedicating my life to a series of meaningful projects, and thereby fixing up my corner of the world, I refine my own character and ultimately achieve a sense of inner peace and fulfillment. That is real happiness.

A MYSTICAL PERSPECTIVE

PHYSICAL PLEASURES DO NOT LAST, or even accumulate. We cannot enjoy the steak today that we ate last night, nor will the next steak we devour taste better because I had one the night before.

Spiritual pleasures, however, do build upon each other. I can grow in my moral values of honesty, kindness and selflessness. Each level of my personal growth stays with me and becomes part of my character.

Maimonides, the 13th century Talmudist and philosopher, explains this concept with following question: Is it better to give one hundred dollars to one person or to give one dollar to one hundred different people? Most of us would certainly think that giving one hundred dollars to one person would make a bigger positive impact on his or her life than many individuals receiving a nominal sum! Isn't the one hundred dollar gift more meaningful?

Well, maybe, but only if you look at charity from the perspective of what it does for the recipient. The purpose of charity, though, is not only to provide for the needy, but also to benefit the giver. Obviously, if God would desire, He could provide everyone with a comfortable living, and without the need for charity. However, He chose not to set up His world that way, in order to challenge both the wealthy and the poor to grow.

As Maimonides puts it, if each of us gives one gift of one hundred dollars to one person, then it is considered that we have performed an act of kindness; but if we each give one dollar to one hundred different people, and have put our hands in our pockets one hundred times, then each one of those times has made a spiritual impact on us. This way, we're not just giving charity, rather we are training ourselves to become more charitable people. We transform our personalities by toning down our natural inclinations to treat everything we have as "mine," and we begin to see ourselves more as a conduit or trustee of our possessions, which we can manage with kindness, and thereby help to develop our personalities. That is what is meant by personal or spiritual growth.

Because we are a combination of horse and rider, body and soul, it's up to us to decide whether our lives will be impulse-or body-driven, or spiritually-soul-driven. The Torah—the Five Books of Moses—in the very first verse of Genesis, gives us guidance as to how we can best fulfill our potential and destiny: "In the beginning God created the Heaven and the Earth." In other words, God created the world with a duality—spirituality and physicality—represented by Heaven and Earth, respectively.

The spiritual dimension is meant to take precedence over the physical dimension. After all, the order of the words in the verse suggests that God first created the Heavens, and only then created then Earth. Through the exercise of our free will, we can choose to be "earth"ly—or physically-oriented, or we can instead elevate our physical dimension by focusing on the spiritual.

This is not to suggest that we deny our physical side. After all, God Himself created both spiritual and the physical aspects of the world, both the soul and body. However, God's very first communication to us sets out this fundamental guideline for humanity: let your spirituality lead your physicality. Let your heavenly dimension guide your earthly dimension.

The soul, as it operates within this world, has three parts to it:

1) *Nefesh*—the animal soul; our physical instincts.

2) *Ruach*—the emotional soul; our appreciation of the aesthetic—art, music, harmony and symmetry.

3) *Neshama*—the intellect; our pursuit of truth, wisdom and values.

Normally, most of us operate on the level of our "*ruach*," our emotional soul. Sometimes we react from our earthy, instinctive, "*nefesh*" selves. Other times, we rise to our first-class "*neshama*," selves, and we allow our higher, intellectual selves to guide us.

God challenges us to choose, through our God-given will, which dimension to live in.

Besides the type of charity where we just donate money, another area for spiritual growth is dedicating our time and energy to a cause outside of our own immediate needs. This kind of work often gives life a sense of purpose and meaning. We can make a major impact on our community by dedicating, for instance, one tenth of our time and energies to community needs, and, at the same time, we will find that it profoundly helps in the development of our own spirituality.

Spiritual growth also applies to other areas of our lives—in "passive" as well as in active ways. What I mean by "passive" is that if we "work on ourselves" by stopping ourselves from just acting instinctively, with knee-jerk reactions to events or comments, we thereby exercise our free will and behave spiritually.

Instead of hiding behind our "natural" state of reacting angrily to a frustrating situation, rationalizing that "that's the way I am," we could choose to do something about the way we instinctively react to life's challenges. In order to do this, though, we need to identify which areas of our personalities need changing and to develop a strategy to modify those behaviors.

The first step is simply to become aware of our reactions, without trying at first to change them. We must try to notice every time we lose our temper or react angrily. We must step out of ourselves at those moments, and watch ourselves from a corner of the room, and observe our reactions.

We also need to watch others interact with us and observe how our behavior affects them. If we see something unpleasant in our actions, we need to ask ourselves how we could handle this situation differently in the future. Learning from our past mistakes and trying to rectify our behavior is acting spiritually. Even if we repeat the same mistake, as long as we are at least trying to control our behavior and improve, we are still being spiritual. Of course, all this takes effort and a tremendous investment of energy. No one said it was going to be easy.

4

BECOMING
OURSELVES

A SPIRITUAL PERSPECTIVE

I NOW KNOW THAT it is my spiritual center that directs my drives, desires and passions. It acts as the decision-making headquarters of my pursuit of inner peace and focuses my abilities towards achieving self-fulfillment. But, since each of us has a different set of strengths and weaknesses, each of us face a different set of challenges. Those challenges shape our unique identities, and bring out the best of our latent and potential qualities.

For me, unless I am pushed to produce, I will usually take the path of least resistance and not produce my best results. It is true that some people do not perform well under pressure. However, many of us simply will not achieve our potential unless we are pressed to the limit of our abilities. That is why we need challenges. When the going gets tough, the tough start thinking:

"This is a challenge tailor-made for me. What strength or weakness in me is being highlighted by the present crisis? I know it is being sent to bring out a better part of me. Let me analyze this challenge and see how I can grow through this experience."

Let's take a look at an example of a challenge that a friend of mine once faced:

This friend is an extremely kind individual. He runs an interest-free loan fund for large families who have a tough time making ends meet. He also gives of his time generously to advise others. One day, his car broke down and he tried to hitch a ride. Many of the people who saw him were people whom he had personally helped, but no one stopped to offer him a ride.

He said to himself, "This is a challenge to my personality. What have I done, perhaps, specifically involving a car, that I am now being tested with this particular challenge?" He searched his memory and reminded himself that there was an elderly man to whom he gave a ride every morning. One particular morning the previous week, he was running late and drove by the elderly man, trying to avoid the time-consuming process of getting him into the car and escorting him up the steps to his apartment. "I knew I should have given him that ride," he said to himself. At that precise second someone stopped to pick him up. He decided that this challenge was sent to him to further develop and refine his quality of kindness.

If I probe seriously into my personality, it may well be possible to identify a correlation between my past actions and a challenge currently being presented to me. However, this may not always be possible. Although I am unable to see a connection, the challenge may still have been sent to me so that I can learn something. I can and should regularly engage in some self-reflection and analysis of my spiritual center, to come up with some aspect of my life where I can improve or develop. But if I haven't found the time or the motivation to do that, a challenge may be presented to me to give me just that motivation.

Let's look at another example, of a challenge sent to help rectify someone's particular weakness:

I know someone who is extremely short-tempered. One day, she came home from a hard day at the office only to find the house a complete mess, dinner nowhere near ready and the kids still not having been picked up from day care. So she said to her husband, "You know I have a short temper, dear. Why is the house always in such a shambles?" So he said, "Don't keep relying on that 'short-tempered' excuse. Why don't you just help me?!" She responded, "Actually, you never explained it like that before. In the past, you've always just yelled back. So, how can I help?"

Whether having a short temper is a genetic condition or a learned behavior doesn't really matter. I may be inclined to anger or a short temper. However, I cannot hide behind that personality trait and just give in to it. Situations will occur to challenge me to work on myself and change my personality to be more even-tempered and understanding. Both of these examples illustrate how challenges can lead to personal growth.

A MYSTICAL PERSPECTIVE

THE FACT IS THAT no one can fully achieve ultimate contentment and tranquility. However, before we give up and throw in the towel, we must try to understand—the reason we can't achieve true contentment is that contentment is the feeling generated by personality growth itself. Each time we grow in character, we gain greater capacity to take on more challenges, and we thereby become more integrated and whole with our life's destiny. Since we are always striving to grow by being more even-tempered, kind and more selfless, our inner feelings of personal satisfaction and inner happiness are always developing, changing and growing as we grow toward actualizing our life's mission. Thus, we are constantly moving from one level of "self" to the next. We reach plateaus of contentment but soon realize that the road to contentment is an incline. We must continue climbing, or we'll start to slide backwards.

There is an often-told story of a saintly teacher named Reb Zusia. He was a great and learned man, pious and charitable—a leader by example. As he grew very old and was nearing his end, his students saw that he became extremely anxious. Questioned by his students as to why a man so pious as Reb Zusia had anything to fear, he said, "I am concerned because I will soon have to give an accounting for my life's actions. Yet I am not worried that the Heavenly Court will ask me, 'Zusia—why were you not like Abraham, Isaac and Jacob?' Nor am I worried that they will ask me why I did not achieve the level of Moses. But I am worried that I won't know what to respond when they ask me, 'Zusia—why were you not like Zusia?'"

Each of us has our own unique potential, based on our unique mix of abilities and weaknesses. We were not meant to achieve the level of anyone else besides ourselves. We are meant, however, to be as exemplary as our own potential allows.

There is another well-known story about a young man who sets out to change the world. After his idealism takes a bit of a battering, he modifies his goals and decides to change only his city. When that too proves to be too ambitious, he decides to change merely his neighborhood. When he finds that impossible, he tries to change just the people on his street. That plan, too, is shelved, and he tries then to change only his own family. Finally, when here too he does not succeed, he decides to change the one person that he can—himself.

Perhaps the young man who set out to change the world in the second story is actually Zusia of the first story. How can we "change the world"? By changing ourselves.

A third story may help to illustrate this idea:

Rabbi Isser Zalman Meltzer was once studying with a student when he heard his wife scream in the kitchen. He rushed in to find his wife staring at the milk which had boiled over on the stove. Knowing that such small daily occurrences didn't usually evoke such an extreme reaction, he asked his wife what was really bothering her. She told him that, when the milk boiled over, she asked herself, "What have I done with milk that God is challenging me in this way?"

She reviewed her day and remembered that she had not had enough money to pay the milkman that day, and concluded that that was why the milk had boiled over. She immediately went down to the milk company and asked to see her milk deliveryman. She was given his home address, went to his house, and handed him the money. His face lit up.

He told her, "I am very poor and get paid by the day. Today, when you couldn't pay me, I did not have enough money for dinner for my family. Now I can pick up some food for my children."

God had sent Mrs. Meltzer a challenge, and she was on the spiritual frequency to pick up the message that God was sending her. Instead of being angry and frustrated, she was able to see this incident as a challenge and turn it into an opportunity for personal growth. She was also fortunate enough to immediately witness the benefits of that growth.

I know what you're thinking: I'm not on the spiritual level of Mrs. Meltzer to be able to figure out the meaning of the events that God sends. First of all, we shouldn't sell ourselves short. If we dig deep into our actions and motivations, we will often be able to figure out a connection. Even if we are not that "in tune" with our spiritual centers to be able to quickly figure out a direct correlation, if we are spiritually-oriented, then whatever event we are examining we can just conclude that God wants us to grow in some area of our lives, and focus on something in ourselves which we can improve. Just finish this sentence: I have always wanted to improve my life by… I can use the particular challenge facing me to address that issue.

Life is a process. The situations presented to us are landmarks along the way and we can chart our progress by responding from our soul's perspective. This is the meaning of Abraham's journey, when God called upon him* to fulfill the directive of "lech lecha"—to leave his homeland, his birthplace, and his father's house, and to go to a land that God would reveal to him. The opening words of this challenge from God are "lech lecha," which mean, "go for yourself." Why doesn't God merely say "Go!"? Why does He say "go for yourself"? What God is instructing Abraham is this: the events you will encounter on your journey, Abraham, will cause you to delve into and get to know your real self.

---

* See Genesis 12:1.

Our souls are sensitized to their live's mission by challenges to each of our own particular strengths and weaknesses. If one of our weaknesses is a lack of sensitivity or consideration for others and we're too selfish and egocentric, then God might challenge us with a physical illness to teach us humility. Then others will have to care for us and we'll have the opportunity to develop our sense of gratitude and become less arrogant. In such a situation, we have the option of reacting to our challenge by being angry with God, or we can step back from our "self" and ask: Is God challenging me to change my attitude? Can I use this experience to become a better person? Being mad at God misses the point of the challenge, and of life.

God personally told Abraham to embark upon his life's journey, and each of us, too, has a God-given mission in life. Each of us, like Abraham, is on a personal journey, inspired, prodded, and guided, by God. The goal or mission of the journey is not usually readily apparent to us. God did not specifically tell Abraham *where* to go. He just said, "to a land that I will show you." That is why part of the mission itself is to take inventory of our personal strengths and weaknesses and see how we can rectify and improve our personality flaws, and how we can develop our strengths. This is our private mission. We also have public missions, though—such as making our own unique contribution to our families, communities and society. We fulfill our public missions by raising children who feel good about themselves and who, in turn, can look positively at fulfilling their own private and public missions. We can also fulfill our public missions through our careers or through community volunteer work.

God presents us with certain life challenges to help us figure out our private and public missions. If we work on this process, then we are engaging and strengthening our relationship with God. Our public and private missions comprise our life's journey. As we go through life and figure out our mission, we reveal our destination—"a land that God will show us." In the process of our journey, we reveal our true selves.

Abraham had to endure ten tests of faith in order to actualize his potential to become the father of the Jewish nation. He had to 1) leave his homeland; 2) endure famine in Canaan; 3) see his wife Sarah kidnapped by Pharoah; 4) fight a war to rescue his nephew; 5) experience childlessness; 6) undergo circumcision at age ninety-nine; 7) have his wife Sarah kidnapped by the king of Gerar; 8) banish his wife Hagar and 9) his son Ishmael; and 10) offer his son Isaac to be sacrificed.

Did God hate Abraham that he tested him with so many painful ordeals? No. God actually loved him and felt he was worth prodding to reach his potential. Rabbi Shalom Noach Brozofsky, who wrote the *Nesivos Shalom*, explains that, like Abraham, each of us endures ten tests during our lifetimes. The tests are all soul-searching tests of our faith in God. I'm on test number six in my life. What test are you on?

5

THE PURPOSE
OF LIFE

A SPIRITUAL PERSPECTIVE

THE PURPOSE OF LIFE is not to see how many times I can remodel my kitchen.

Are you sure?

Positive. The purpose of life is really twofold. First, my private purpose—to develop my character to become the best person I can be. The measure of my life's growth is how much I have developed and transformed my personality from infancy to old age. If I am an angry person, then my task is to become more calm and even-tempered. If I am miserly, then my mission is to become more charitable and giving. If I am so meek that people walk all over me, then my mission is to learn to stand up for myself. My second purpose in life—my public purpose—is what I do, with my abilities, to improve my corner of the world.

A MYSTICAL PERSPECTIVE

HOW DO WE KNOW which of our strengths we are meant to develop, and which of our weaknesses we are meant to rectify?

Well, there are two possible leading indicators to follow: first, if there is an issue which keeps coming up in our lives, over and over again, then we must realize that this issue is our personal issue to be worked on. For example, if you are always late, and it really upsets you that you're always late, but you can still never quite "get your act together," then clearly one of your purposes in life is to rectify that particular trait. If you're miserly, and it really bothers you why you can't be more charitable, then that must be one of the issues that need to be rectified.

Second, the issue must be one which really gets to you, and which affects you to the core of your being. In other words, the issue has to make you say: This is mind-blowing. You feel so deeply about the issue because your life force—your soul—is stirred by it. Your life force is God's ambassador in this world—and listening to its messages is one way to engage in a personal relationship with Him.

For example, if you're a computer programmer, but you don't find computer programming fulfilling, and you spend your evenings and weekends writing creative short stories, or if you go to work every weekday morning with a frustrated feeling in your heart, knowing that you could be a good writer and that it would bring you fulfillment, then you know that this is your "issue" and that you have to work out a plan to give expression to your life goal and ambition.

We must, however, state two important cautionary points. First, even if you identify "your issue" and you determine that you want to make a major life change in career or studies or personality, you must act responsibly when other people are involved, i.e., your spouse, children and associates. You cannot simply change jobs and become an artist, for example, when you have no way to support or finance your family. You must think, reflect, discuss and plan a strategy for this major change that you now have found the hidden strength to actualize.

Second, you don't have to change your life goals overnight. You can ease into a major change by taking a course or giving a lecture, or by starting to write that book or paint that landscape. Start slow and let the answer evolve. But start.

The psychologist's philosophy of "if it feels good then do it," does not apply when you are dealing with major life decisions and changes. The introspection and reflection that you must do in order to get in touch with your true feelings takes place over time, sometimes months or even years. It is and it must be a process that evolves within you as you go through life's experiences. Each new event and experience molds and shapes your mind and contributes to the transformation process that goes on within your soul. The crucial thing is to be able to "take your own pulse" by delving into your inner self, in order to guide yourself in the decision making process.

Once you identify your purpose in life, then you can initiate a new process—that of actualizing or achieving it. The introspection to identify your purpose and the striving and pursuit of achieving it puts you on the track toward real or "inner" happiness. Happiness is the by-product of dedicating your life to a series of valuable and worthwhile projects. I say "series," because once you embark upon the process of identifying and actualizing your mission or missions, new doors or opportunities will then open up along the way. You have to keep your eyes open and your spiritual center alert, in order to see, hear, and most importantly, "feel" the new doors as they open.

6

LET'S GET GOING

A SPIRITUAL PERSPECTIVE

WHEN THE ALARM GOES off at 6 A.M., I often suffer a little bereavement at the "loss" of my precious sleep.

In fact, I actually undergo the same four-step process that psychologists say takes place upon the unfortunate loss of a loved one, namely: denial, shock, anger and acceptance.

Stage 1: Denial

Can it really be morning already? I just fell asleep an hour ago! Say it ain't so! See, it's still dark outside... I must have set the alarm wrong. This is a dream, right? Then I check my watch: 6:02 A.M. This can't be happening... Enter stage 2...

Stage 2: Shock

I tossed and turned all night and now I have to leave the curled-up warmth of the fetal position and face the cold realities of life. How can I cope with the rat race on two hours of sleep?

Stage 3: Anger

I hate my job. I hate my boss. I hate this city. I hate my life! Why do I have to work for a living? Why can't I just manage someone's stock portfolio?

Stage 4: Acceptance

Okay, calm down. I'll take a shower. I'll feel better. Get a grip!

I get dressed, resigned to the reality of a new day. I get into the car and set my mind in gear. Here we go again. Just two hundred and seventy-eight days to my summer vacation. Hang in there!

This daily routine can really get me down. It makes me tense, irritable and anxious. Every day I experience the same inner turmoil and struggle. I get up each morning wishing it were Saturday. I hope today won't be worse than yesterday. I wish I could shake this routine and get out of this rut. There is a way, I know. I can get out of this routine, but it is up to me—and my attitude.

ↄ ↄ ↄ

A couple of years ago I was going through a rough patch, feeling sorry for myself, playing the victim and seeking sympathy. I felt stuck in a rut and was unable to see the light at the end of the tunnel. A close friend of mine wouldn't stand for it.

He advised me, "When you are ready to come out of this, you will. It's up to you."

I resisted. "It's not my fault. It's these circumstances that are beyond my control that are getting me down. Right?"

Wrong, I eventually realized. Circumstances are neutral. They're just there. How I react to them is up to me.

So, instead of going through my daily "I hate the world, and life's not fair" syndrome, all I really need is to change my attitude. Sure I'm exhausted and drained. Everyone is. Still, I must remember the "purpose of life," which is… to get out of bed in the morning, in order to keep growing and developing into the person that I am supposed to become.

To keep growing, I must keep going. Instead of the morning alarm clock getting me down, I could choose to hear the alarm music as a personal challenge—you can do this! You can take charge of your life. Just rise to the challenge. You can make decisions today that will change your life for the better. You can turn your life into an adventure. So get your act together, and work "with" the world instead of "against" it.

A MYSTICAL PERSPECTIVE

IN ONE OF THEIR SONGS, the Beatles wrote, "I get by with a little help from my friends." If we opened our eyes this morning, that obviously means that our "Friend" upstairs wanted us to. We didn't have to wake up this morning. Many people haven't. Obviously, if God wants us to be players in His world today, then our waking is the ultimate vote of confidence. God has reactivated our souls because He feels that we can achieve something today. If God believes in us, then don't we have the right, in fact the obligation, to believe in ourselves?

So, a good way to get motivated in the morning is to say a little personal prayer after the alarm goes off. "Thank you God for giving me a new day, a new opportunity to enjoy life and to show my stuff." In fact, those are, in effect, the first words a Jew says in the morning, in morning prayers, "I gratefully thank You God, O Living and Eternal King, for restoring my soul to me this morning; *rabah emunasecha*—abundant is Your faithfulness."

Isn't there a mistake in this prayer? "Abundant is Your faithfulness" seems to suggests that God is the One Who has faith. Aren't *we* the ones who are supposed to have faith in God? Who does God have faith in?

The answer must be that God actually has faith in… ME! He proved it by restoring my life energy to me this morning. He did so because He has confidence in each of us that we have the potential to accomplish great things today. We can take a step toward accomplishing these things by beginning to activate our "self" in the morning.

The best way for each one of us to activate our "self" is by becoming aware of it. In general, in relationships, we do this by acknowledging and recognizing another person's existence. In our relationship with God, recognizing God as a real entity, rather than as a theoretical concept, puts us in a mindset to begin relating to Him directly. This acknowledgment also brings with it a sense of humility and gratitude that reminds us that we did not create ourselves, but that we receive our life energy from a source outside of ourselves. That source is our Creator.

This morning He re-created us, and now each one of us has to ask how we can begin to re-create ourselves. When we start our day with this type of personal gratitude prayer, then we can put ourselves into a positive mindset and start our day with enthusiasm.

This is not just another mind game. Imagine, for instance, a man who is terminally ill. He is told that he only has a few months left to live. He puts his affairs in order, goes through a painful course of treatment and prepares for the end. After a few months the doctors are astonished at his test results and tell him that he will survive. How does he feel at that moment? Like the happiest man alive! Literally. No one is happier. He is going to live!

So, what does he have that you and I don't have? He has life and we have life. The difference lies only in his *attitude*, in his appreciation of life. He appreciates every breath, every sound, every flower. We don't. We have become desensitized to the wonder that is life. We take it for granted. If only we were able to feel like that man, and live on that level every day. Our lives—every moment of it—would take on new meaning. We could literally appreciate every time we opened our eyes in the morning as a sweet new opportunity to recreate ourselves.

HIDDEN
STRENGTH

A SPIRITUAL PERSPECTIVE

WHEN THE CHIPS ARE DOWN and my back is against the wall, don't I almost always pull through? I need to remember that when faced with my next crisis. I must tell myself: "You can do this. You've been here before."

How can I be so sure?

Because I wouldn't have been given this test if the purpose was to destroy me. I was given this test so that I can grow personally through the experience, either by meeting the challenge and solving it, or by learning to cope with, endure or live with my inability to solve it. Either way it was something I *had* to go through in order to develop myself, by developing my spiritual center.

Where do I find the strength to keep going? Where do I find

the resolve to get through it?

I take a deep breath, and then I dig deep into my spiritual center, and take an inventory of my strengths, talents and abilities, which are already present within my psyche and personality. I remind myself that I have been endowed with the inner abilities to solve the problem. All I have to do is think about the issue and determine which talents I need to utilize. So when the going gets tough, the tough get thinking about personal strengths and resources. Self-awareness is a prerequisite for self-esteem. So once I know the stuff my "self" is made of, then I can start activating my "self" by adopting a positive "I can do this" attitude.

A MYSTICAL PERSPECTIVE

OUR NATURAL REACTION TO yet another crisis (this is the third one today and its only 10:30 in the morning!) is: "I have had it! I can't handle this! How much can one person take?" Sound familiar? Well, we've all said it, and, for the most part, we've survived to tell the tale. Doesn't that tell us something? We're more capable than we think. We can do it—it's only a question of attitude.

When Hagar, the concubine of Abraham, was in the desert with her son Ishmael and feared for his life because of the lack of water, the Torah states: "God 'opened her eyes' and she saw a well of water; and she went and she filled the water flask and she gave the boy to drink" (Genesis 21:9). The Torah does not say that God performed a miracle and created a well for her in the desert. The Torah is teaching us here that Hagar's mind and eyes had been closed to the possibility of saving her child—so she had been unable to "see" the well that was already there. Her anxiety closed her soul from the creative thinking that problem solving requires.

The Talmud says that God sends the antidote before He sends the illness (*Megillah* 13b). One of the ramifications of this concept is that God has already placed within us the latent ability to deal with our issues, crises and challenges. Our problem is that we often tend to despair and get into a negative mode, which clouds our vision and prevents us from activating our innate abilities to deal with the problem, and from transforming our abilities from potential to actual.

When Moses first encountered God at the burning bush, he entered into a seven-day-long "discussion" with God, with Moses arguing that he was the wrong man for the job to take the Jews out of Egypt, and God insisting that he was the right man.

God pointed out, however, that Egypt was the strongest nation on earth at that time, that Pharaoh wouldn't listen to Moses because He, God, would harden Pharaoh's heart, and that the Jewish People were a stubborn, "stiff-necked" people and it was mighty hard to be their leader. Despite all that, God told Moses to do it anyway, "for I am with you."

We would probably agree that Moses was at least a little justified in wanting to refuse the job. Isn't there, in fact, a little bit of Moses in all of us? When faced with a daunting, formidable problem, don't we all say what Moses, our Teacher said?—"I can't handle this. Please send somebody else!"

The answer lies in the manner in which God revealed Himself to Moses, and first commissioned him for the job. God said: "*Al tikrav halom, ki hamakom asher atah omed alav, admas kodesh hu*—do not come any nearer, for the place upon which you stand is holy ground" (Exodus 3:5).

There seems to be a mistake in this verse. God should have said, Don't come any closer, because the place where *I, God,* stand—is holy ground. I am the One who solves the incredible contradiction of "the burning bush that is not consumed." Where God was and is—that is holy ground.

Why did God say, "For the place upon which *you* stand is holy ground?" As is usually the case, the answer rests within the question. God was telling Moses that the task that He was giving him was fraught with contradictions—like the burning bush itself. Nevertheless, Moses *would* succeed, because the place upon which he stood was already holy ground, by virtue of the potential that already existed within him. God was telling him: You don't have to come closer to the bush to reach holiness. You can reach holiness from where you stand right now. Just activate your potential, Moses.

So you see here that the timeless Torah says to the Moses that is within every one of us, to every Jew who is faced with a burning problem or a contradiction in life: You can solve the problem—because I, God, have sent the contradiction, and I sent it to you because you *can* and *must* deal with it, for your own personal growth. If our life situations are difficult, it is precisely from within and through those situations that God desires our *avodah,* our service. Our mission is to respond to God's challenge with the words, "*Hineni*—I am here, and ready to serve You!"

We can meet and deal with each of our crises because God tailor-makes each crisis so that we can activate our already existing—albeit sometimes dormant—strengths. God does not give us problems to break us. He directs, controls and chooses each circumstance presented to every individual, and each individual circumstance is necessary for that person's growth in character.

Each of us is called upon to give the best possible response that we are capable of offering. This is all that God expects of us. That does not mean that we will necessarily be able to overcome every crisis or challenge, and see every problem through to a happy resolution. The best possible response may simply mean that we are able to withstand the difficulty, live with the condition or situation, and come to terms with our inability to solve the problem. Sometimes, however, we are unable to achieve even this, and then it becomes clear that what we are going through is not a test but a type of challenge. We'll discuss that in the next chapter.

8

GIVE ME A BREAK

YOU KNOW THE FEELING—exhaustion, frayed nerves, a fresh cereal stain on the suit jacket that you just picked up from the cleaners, courtesy of your adorable six-month-old son, financial pressure, kids who go to sleep at midnight and get up at 5:30 A.M., that young guy at work who gets a promotion over you… and the ultimate anguish—the modem isn't working! You feel like packing it all in, throwing in the towel, and just giving up. And as if someone is listening, you cry out: "Give me a break!"

Well, you're in good company. We all feel that way from time to time. Okay, a lot of the time. And that's… good.

Thanks a lot! How is that good?!

It's good because you are supposed to be pushed to the limits of your strength and abilities, fortitude and patience. Why?

Because, if you think about it, you'll realize that when your back is up against the wall, you usually do find the strength to weather the storm. In fact, you do more than merely "weather" the difficulty, you actually excel. You even surprise yourself as to how well you handled it. You didn't know your own strength! Exactly. Your dormant abilities were activated by the challenge and you were able to handle the situation.

But isn't it true that when the chips are down you usually deliver? In a personal or family crisis, or when a friend needs emotional support, or even a loan, you do come through. You may ask yourself: "Did I really agree to that? I said what?! What was I thinking? I can't do that!" But these statements are said after the fact. In truth, you did say that you would help, that you would commit to that particular responsibility. You did come through in the heat of the moment. Which feeling truly represents reality? The commitment you made in the "eye of the storm," or your sober "what have I done?" reflections afterward?

Think about it. When confronted with a crisis situation, you'll discover that you usually respond with the noblest part of yourself, from deep within your spiritual center. Isn't it true that the crisis brings out the best in you? When there is a moment of need, you rise to the occasion. You are pushed beyond what you thought were the limits of your personality and abilities, and you succeed. But it is only as a result of being pressed to the wall that you find out what you can really accomplish. It is due to the crisis that you go that extra yard, and reveal how truly good you are inside. Except that now… the good is on the outside. More good has been brought into the world, and more of you—*the real you*—has been revealed. All because of a challenge.

A MYSTICAL PERSPECTIVE

THE PATRIARCH IN THE Torah with whom people often find it easiest to identify with is Jacob. He had it tough in life. Jacob's brother, Esau, threatened his life, so Jacob fled to his uncle's house. On the way, Esau's son stole all his money. He didn't see his parents for twenty-two years. His uncle Laban repeatedly tricked him, and switched his contract of employment one hundred times. He worked seven years for the right to marry Rachel, only to be tricked into marrying Leah. His daughter, Dinah, was raped. His favorite son, Joseph, was thought dead for twenty-two years. Finally, after all this upheaval and turmoil, the Torah states: *"Vayeshev Yaakov b'eretz megurei aviv, b'eretz Canaan*—And Jacob dwelled in the land of the sojourns of his father, in the land of Canaan" (Genesis 37:1).

The *Midrash* on this verse comments on the words, "And Jacob 'sat'"—Jacob wanted to "sit down" and rest, to which God's response was, "is it not enough that I have set aside a place for the righteous to rest in the World to Come? Yet Jacob wants to rest in tranquility in this world too?!"

Jacob was basically saying to God: "Give me a break!" Life's been tough enough! Can't I just rest from my troubles and turmoil—just a bit? God, however, would have none of it. God knew that Jacob's job in this world was to be "Yisroel"—which meant he was to strive with God and with men, and prevail. That is why, after Jacob won a wrestling match with the angel, God gave Jacob the additional name "Yisroel."

Our task, as well, is to face and wrestle with challenges, and to prevail over ourselves, and transform ourselves into a new level of "self" in the process. Just like each of Jacob's crises were

Heaven-sent, so is each of ours.

Jacob's son, Joseph, didn't have it much easier than his father. He experienced tremendous highs and lows in his journey through life. Joseph dreamt of the eleven stars, the sun and moon bowing down to him as king. A few weeks later he was sold into slavery to traveling Ishmaelites, who in turn sold him to an Egyptian nobleman. A little while later, he found himself in charge of the Egyptian nobleman's household. Just as things seemed to be turning around for him and his "career" prospects were looking up, he found himself tossed into an Egyptian jail, falsely accused of attempted rape, where he languished for twelve years. Finally, he was given the opportunity to interpret the dreams of Pharaoh, and, after successfully doing so, he became the viceroy of Egypt.

Talk about ups and downs! How did Joseph handle that roller-coaster ride? The answer lies in Joseph's attitude, which we can discern in his reactions throughout all his travails.

When Joseph was a servant in the household of Potiphar, the Egyptian nobleman, the Torah states about him, "His master saw that God was with him, and that all he would do God would make successful in his hand" (Genesis 39:3).

Rashi, the 11th century Biblical commentator, remarks on the words, "that God was with him"—The name of Heaven was always on Joseph's lips, which means that he would regularly refer to God in conversation as the source of his success. When he was in jail and interpreted the dreams of the butler and the baker, Joseph said, do not interpretations belong to God? He felt he was merely a messenger or mouthpiece of God in interpreting the dreams. When he was asked by Pharaoh to interpret his dream, he replied, "It is beyond me; *God* will respond to

Pharaoh's request" (Genesis 41:16).

The lesson Joseph was teaching us was that our outlook in life should be that whatever happens in life is from God, and can be dealt with through trusting that God is guiding us.

There is an important principle that the more we believe in Divine Providence—that is, in an ongoing, dynamic relationship with God—the more God's clear and direct guidance will be shown to us. The more we relate to God, the more God will relate to us.

What we need to understand is that there are actually three phases in the development of the "self." First, there is self-awareness—becoming aware of our unique identity. We must learn to appreciate "being," not just "doing." Second, we must learn to like the "self" that we are; we must develop a sense of self-esteem. And finally, through life's challenges, we must become the best person we can, by journeying on the path of self-discovery through personal growth.

When do the challenges end, you may ask? Not in this world. They're not meant to. This world is a world of non-stop challenges and tests, presented to us by God in order to persuade, inspire and push us to move up a level in character refinement. That is the purpose of this world. In the next world, we can rest and reflect and live in the person we have become—forever. But until then, we must occupy ourselves with the process.

The World to Come is also called the Garden of Eden, which is comprised of "trees." A tree represents the concept of "process." The bark and trunk of the tree and the tree's internal system work hard to produce the result—the fruit. The Torah tells us that, in the original Garden of Eden, "*eitz p'ri oseh p'ri*— the tree produced fruit unique to its species" (Genesis 1:11).

Rashi comments that the words, *"eitz p'ri,"* which mean "fruit tree" meant that the bark of the tree was originally intended to taste like the fruit of the tree, that the tree was equivalent to the fruit.

What does this mean? It means that the process of creating the fruit—i.e., the travail, crises and ordeals of life, is itself that which produces the "fruit," i.e., the development of the self. And in the Garden of Eden, the tree—that is, the "process," tastes just like the fruit, which means that the difficult tree process—the process that produces the fruit—is itself the reward.

In the World to Come, we will realize and reflect upon all our travails in this world—the tree process—and see how each crisis helped develop us into the characters and personalities that we became—the fruit.

In this world, we see the tree and fruit as two separate things—the difficulties are distinct from the reward. In the World to Come, we will realize that it was all one and the same. The tree, the travail, becomes as tasty as the outcome—the fruit itself. And we will live in our fully developed "selves"—in the Garden of Eden forever.

That doesn't mean that we should ask for tests and challenges in life. We don't need to; they'll come on their own. But if we are able to step back from the particular ordeal we are currently facing and put it into perspective, we might be able to see the forest from the trees, both the tree and the fruit, and be better able to handle the current crisis.

Now, you might be wondering: What about people who do appear broken by life's ordeals? Doesn't God only send us ordeals that we are capable of handling? So why do some people appear as if they really can't handle the tragedy of their lives?

According to Rabbi Eliyahu Dessler, there are two types of "*mazal*" or destinies. There is *mazal tachton*—a "this-world" destiny, which can be changed through prayer, personal growth and kind deeds—all of which we activate through the exercise of our free will. A crisis sent to us under the rubric of *mazal tachton* is a test to be solved or withstood and seen to a successful conclusion. However, there are other types of challenges sent to us from *mazal elyon*, which represent our "beyond this world" destiny, and they are not meant for us to solve, but are meant solely to be endured. They are sent to us because our souls need them in order to receive their *tikun*, their ultimate rectification.

Sure, you might be inclined to say, "I'll do without the spiritual refinement, God. Please, just give me situations I can handle!" We need to accept, though, that God knows better than we do what's best for our souls. Though the difficulty may seem unbearable, it is exactly what the soul needs to achieve its ultimate *tikun*, which will last forever.

God is willing to deal with the bad press. He does whatever is necessary in order to bring about the total refinement of our souls, even if it means that some may question His intentions. That's how God shows His love for us. We may have to endure some bitter medicine in this world, but the long-term results are worth it. Forever, after all, is a long time.

9

RESPONDING TO SUFFERING

A SPIRITUAL PERSPECTIVE

THERE IS AN ADVERTISEMENT from the Israeli Tourism Office that shows a photograph of a desert scene with one, lone, red, prickly flower growing on a thorn bush, with the caption: "We never promised you a rose garden."

When things get tough in my life, I sometimes say to myself: What's going on here? Am I not entitled to a little happiness? Why are there so many valleys and deserts in my life? And then I get angry and depressed, which affects those around me and puts them in a depressed mood as well, based on the prevailing theory that if I am miserable, then everyone else needs to be miserable too.

There is a better way. Life is *not* just about living through suffering. The key to successful living is to respond to the challenges of life, and to grow from them. The bottom line is that it is my attitude that will set the tone of my life. And my attitude is completely up to me. Am I going to live my life allowing external events and stimuli to take me where they want? Am I going to let life just "happen," or am I going to take charge and deal with my life proactively? Am I going to allow my life to be defined by my ordeals—or am I going to define my life as a person who grows through and above and beyond my ordeals.

The secret to maintaining an inner calm in the midst of the storms—okay, hurricanes, okay, tidal waves—of life is to put myself into the proper "response" mode rather than living on autopilot. If I want to succeed at this particular challenge, I must learn that my problems do not define who I am. They exist apart from me. My job is to respond to my problems.

I must strengthen my inner resolve and encourage myself to maintain emotional stamina and a balanced inner emotional state so that I can make considered responses to the "questions" that life poses to me.

Ultimately, I am responsible for the mood and the mode in which I am going to live my life. Life is not meant to be a rose garden and I am not "entitled" to an easy life. My job is to respond to life's challenges and weed the garden, and maybe even plant a few new flowers of my own. This garden of life is mine to cultivate as I wish. I've been given the plot of land and the seeds. The landscaping is up to me.

A MYSTICAL PERSPECTIVE

ONE OF THE FIRST MITZVOT in the Torah following the

account of the giving of the Torah on Mount Sinai is *"eved ivri,"* the laws of the Jewish "slave" (Exodus 21:2). A thief's punishment was to repay at least double the value of the stolen goods, but if his assets could not cover that amount, then he was required to sell the value of his work to pay off his debt. The Jewish "slave" was therefore not really a slave, but more of an employee—and a well provided for employee at that!

The Torah, written over thirty-three hundred years ago, mandated a benefits package for the *eved ivri* of which even today's most powerful unions would be jealous. Just by way of example:

෴ The employer had to provide for the family of his slave/employee.

෴ If the employer had steak, the slave/employee also had to have steak.

෴ If the employer had only one pillow, he had to give it to his slave/employee.

No wonder the Talmud says, "He who acquires a Hebrew slave, acquires for himself a master" (*Kiddushin* 22a).

When the slave paid off his debt with the value of his work, or worked for a maximum of six years, he then went free, unless he chose to continue working for his master/employer.

We often hear the anguished question: Is the destiny of the Jewish People to suffer? Genocide, pogroms, inquisitions… are we, the "Chosen People", chosen only to suffer? The Torah, by teaching us the mitzvah of *eved ivri* as the first mitzvah after the giving of the Torah, is teaching us that Judaism stands not for the faith of the suffering, but for the faith that *responds* to suffering. The practice of enslaving another human being, becoming master over another life, is not Judaism's idea of the fullest expression of human potential. It must be carried out with as much dignity as possible, since it curtails the free will of the enslaved, who is beholden to the will of his master. And with limited free will, his self-esteem is at risk. The Torah ideal is emancipation, not suffering, so slaves were mandated to be freed after six years, and that was thirty-three hundred years ago! In contrast, the United States extended freedom to its slaves only when they were faced with no choice but to do so, after a tragic civil war. Not to mention the slavery and slave labor wages that continue in many places around the world today.

When things get tough, our emotional state may turn to despair and anguish. We may begin to think, why does everyone else have it so easy? Why always me, God? Am I chosen only to live from one problem to the next? Don't we find ourselves repeating, "I know we are the Chosen People, God. But," in the immortal words of Tevye, the milkman, from *Fiddler on the Roof*, "Once in a while can't you choose someone else?"

The answer, though, does not lie in the challenge that God sends to us. The answer lies in our *response* to the challenge. God is not trying to destroy or break us. God does not hate us, nor is He rejecting us. Instinctively, we feel that the opposite is true, but there is also another way of looking at it.

When a parent scolds a child, does it mean that the parent hates his or her child? Not as long as the parent scolds out of love, not anger. The Torah says clearly, "you should know in your heart that just as a father will chastise his son, so Hashem, your God, chastises you" (Deuteronomy 8:5).

The Torah commentary of the *Avi Ezer** explains that God chastises us in order for us to achieve *"shleimus"*—personal

---

* Written in the 18th century by Rabbi Shlomo Hakohen of Lissa.

growth and perfection. God is our parent. As children, we often feel that our parents are just "being mean" to us when they deny us something we want, when in reality they are just looking out for our own safety and well being. God, too, might refuse us that certain new car—because maybe the financial burden would be too much for us, or maybe He feels that old '72 Chevy will keep us more humble. But it still won't do any good to throw a tantrum in the middle of the store. When we learn to control ourselves even though we might not always get what we want, we will have entered into that rarefied state called being "grown up".

Personally, I too sometimes have difficulty saying no to my kids when they want something that "all their friends have" (which really means two friends out of twenty). I worry that I might alienate my child if I say no. In actuality, though, after I do say no, I am amazed to find that they still hug me warmly. The truth is that very deep down, they want me to say no sometimes, because they want boundaries. They want to know that someone is in charge and is looking after them and guiding them, in good times and bad. When they calm down, I sometimes say: "You know why I had to say no or why I had to discipline you?" And they will often say: "Because you want to teach me good *midos* (values)." That's exactly how we can respond to God's saying no to us.

We also have to learn to deal with imperfections in life, and accept that sometimes, for all our efforts to respond successfully to a challenge, we will still fail. Even Adam and Eve couldn't get it right, not even for one full day. They ate from the Tree of Knowledge of Good and Evil on the very day they were created.

The Jewish people, after having received the Torah at Mount Sinai, couldn't keep up their level of perfection for longer than forty days. As a result, they often endured harsh consequences in order to learn from their mistakes.

Just as they were not able to maintain that high level of perfection, we have to understand that it is not expected of us to be perfect; rather, we are to focus on making our personal contribution to the development of spirituality, both for ourselves and for the world. Adam, Eve, and the Jewish People at Sinai may have failed, but their failures did not wipe out the successes they achieved. Adam and Eve still maintained their faith in God despite their failings, and the Jewish nation continued to seek a relationship with God, despite their whopper of a mistake with the Golden Calf.

And that's a big lesson for us too. We make mistakes and have to live with the results, but that does not neutralize all of the good that we accomplish in God's eyes. Look at the big picture—life may not be perfect with its suffering and difficulties, but if we grow through them we come closer to refining our personalities. That gives rise to a sense of inner accomplishment—the essence of real happiness.

10

LIFE'S NOT
TOO SHORT

A SPIRITUAL PERSPECTIVE

LIFE IS TOO short, right?

Not really.

But there's never enough time in the day to…

Actually, there is.

But no one ever achieves *all* of their dreams and aspirations…

Well, actually, they can.

Prove it.

Life is only too short if you don't take full advantage of every opportunity. Life is only too short if you look at life as a series of chores and burdens; then you haven't got enough time to enjoy life. If all your time is spent moaning, complaining, and playing the victim of this or that injustice, then it's true—life is too short.

There is no time to enjoy life because you waste so much time and drain your energy with worry and self-pity. However, you can choose to make life longer and richer for yourself if you look at each experience as an opportunity for learning and growing. Every moment can be full of energy and meaning when you adopt this attitude.

When I would officiate at a wedding, as I did most Sundays as the rabbi of the New West End Synagogue in London, couples would often ask me whether videos were allowed to be taken of the wedding service. "Of course," I would answer, "but you don't really need one. Let me explain—and save you a lot of money."

At many a wedding, the father of the bride would often take me aside right after the veiling ceremony and right before the *chuppah*, the marriage ceremony, and say, "Rabbi, I am about to walk my daughter down the aisle, and I don't know where all the time has gone. Just yesterday I was teaching her how to ride a bike; she was six... and today she's getting married! How is it that I've missed her growing up?"

I'll tell you (but I wouldn't tell him), that the reason he missed his daughter's growing up is that he didn't take the time to appreciate the moments of her life as they were happening. On her first day at school, when she got her first fancy dress, or on her graduation, he would say, "that's nice," without really paying attention to any of it. So time would fly by, and he would miss her growing up and it all became a big blur.

What I would say to brides and grooms is this: When you walk down the aisle, take a snapshot of the moment—*with your mind*. Become aware of what you are doing, appreciate the moment, and make it part of you. If you do that, you won't need a digital camera or a VCR. You will be able to look within yourself, and re-experience the feeling by going to the place within your psyche where "walking down the aisle" resides.

When people go on vacation, even before they actually experience the sight of that beautiful mountain or the Mona Lisa or the waterfall, they're often ready with the camera and snapping pictures. Been there, done that, bought the t-shirt.

But did they *really* see or experience the place? Did they live in the moment and *feel* it? They were there in body—just to say, yeah, I was there, but were they *really* there?

Many people go through life this way. I'm a tourist passing through, so I better take all the photos. They take a video of their children's first steps or their Bar or Bat Mitzvahs, but they don't actually feel or live in the moment. They may seize it on film, but not in their spiritual center. In this way, life can imitate the movies—just a flurry of activity flashing before our eyes—with very little real living involved. When you live life this way, life can be too short. But it doesn't have to be.

A MYSTICAL PERSPECTIVE

AS THE RABBI OF THE New West End synagogue I used to officiate at approximately fifty weddings a year. Invariably, I would be called upon to counsel couples and their families on issues like "this one won't come to the wedding," or "I don't talk to that one," or "they can't be in the same room together because they'll… let's just say it will ruin the wedding." You know, the usual family "*broiges*" (a colorful Yiddish word for aggravations).

How do these quarrels begin and why do they develop into "I haven't spoken to my brother for twenty years" situations?

Usually when we delve into the original disagreements, we often find in hindsight that the issue was extremely insignificant. In the heat of the moment, however, it seemed like it was the end of the world. Like—"I haven't spoken to my sister in twenty years because she sat me next to the kitchen at her son's wedding when I should have been at the head table. After all, I'm her only sister, and Mom and Dad would have been horrified at how she treated me, if they only knew..." Exactly. If they only knew that you were not speaking over something that is so trivial, which makes no difference to the real issues in life... you're right, it's better they don't know.

When a little dispute remains unresolved, it begins to take on a life of its own. We start bringing up old issues. "Mom always loved you best" and "remember that time you didn't lend me..." In psychotherapy it's called "keeping a moral ledger." There is nothing the offending party can do to pay off his or her emotional debt to you. Anger and pain fester in our hearts. No wonder we feel that life's too short. These things zap our strength, and drain all the enjoyment out of our lives. The cycle of recriminations escalates and soon can't be broken without outside intervention, and who wants to get involved in these messes? "I won't touch that one with a ten foot..."

Okay, so let the Torah get involved. In the Torah, God said, "*Lo sisna es acheecha bilvavecha*—do not hate your brother in your heart" (Leviticus 19:17). God is always willing to get involved. He tells us: don't keep the problem in your heart; don't let it fester and become part of your heart, mindset and attitude. Confront it, deal with it, get it out of your heart and into the open. When it is "in your heart," you view things subjectively. You see it only your way—but we must all be humble enough to realize that we don't have a monopoly on the truth.

☙ The invitation was lost in the mail.

☙ I wasn't ignoring you. My mind was on other things, and I just didn't see you.

☙ You were at the head table, but the caterer switched it at the last moment, and I didn't realize it until three-quarters of the way through the meal.

Really? You mean you didn't intend to hurt my feelings? You mean we haven't spoken for all these years just because of a simple misunderstanding?

Life is too short... but it doesn't have to be. So let's pick up the phone, go knock on that door, and get it out in the open. Let's break the cycle, and we'll all live longer.

In the *Shema Yisroel* prayer that a Jew recites twice a day declaring his or her faith in God as the source of life, it says that in the merit of keeping the commandments, God will reward us by "prolonging our days." Now, why would God resort to such a juvenile carrot-on-a-stick reward system—do this and I'll give you long life? Isn't that a primitive and overly simplified outlook on life?

The answer is that "prolonging your days" in this context does not only mean a long life but one that has "breadth of days"—a meaningful life. If we dedicate our lives to meaningful and purposeful projects, then each day will be prolonged. Each day will be filled with meaning.

Before I became a rabbi I practiced law in Toronto. One afternoon, the secretaries in the office were discussing what they would do if they won the lottery. One said she would travel, one said she would buy a log cabin in the woods, and another said she would start a mortgage lending business. Then they asked me what I would do, and I said that I would take some time off to finish my studies and become a rabbi. My senior partner overheard this conversation (it seems that no one was working that day) and said to me, "If you really want to become a rabbi, you should do it. Money should be no object." I froze. He was right. If this was my life's dream, then how could I continue without going for it, without trying to accomplish my dream? How could I live with myself if I wasn't true to my soul? I got home that night and shared this conversation with my wife, and that very night we started talking about my career change. Eventually we moved to Jerusalem so that I could finish my rabbinical studies. I had begun to add more meaning to my life... and soon my life wasn't so short after all.

At the end of our lives, we will invariably look back and lament all the time we wasted. We'll say, "I wish I could have a few more days or minutes and I would live life to the fullest." As Queen Anne put it on her deathbed, "All of my possessions... for a little more time."

One of the most compelling thoughts I had, when I was considering leaving my law practice to follow my dream, was the regret I would have at the end of my life if I chose not to add this experience to my life's adventure. I thereby figuratively projected myself into my eighties, and turned to my projected elderly wife and said, remember that time that we had the chance to go to study in Israel? I wish we'd had the guts to do it. If only we'd had the courage. With these thoughts in mind, I transported myself back to the present and told my senior partner at the firm that I was leaving; then we packed our bags for a life-enhancing experience of studying for the rabbinate in Jerusalem. I will always retain that "breadth of days." I can even, when I so choose, relive those moments by going there in my mind. No photos, no videos, no regrets.

The brilliant American philosopher and author, Henry D. Thoreau, said: "All men lead lives of quiet desperation." I am not about to allow myself to be part of the statistic. I want to make my life count. Here's how you can wake up and smell the spiritual coffee. The Torah states: "*Mipnei seivah takum*—before an old person, arise" (Leviticus 19:32). The Zohar comments on the verse by telling us to put a comma after the word "*seivah*—an old person." So, you would read it like this: "Before an old person, arise," which means, before you *become* an old person—get up and do that which you always dreamed of. As Hillel said, "If not now, when?" (Ethics of the Fathers 1:14).

11

PERSONAL INVENTORY

A SPIRITUAL PERSPECTIVE

SOMETIMES I GET INTO A reflective mood. It may last a day, a week, or a month. I think that what prompts these periods of introspection is that my spiritual center may be stirring, creating within me a discordance between what I am currently doing and what my spiritual center is yearning for. I then have to make sure that I am simply not accepting my current situation by default as being the right choice for my spiritual fulfillment. So I must engage in a personal inventory of my strengths and weaknesses. The best thing for me to do is actually sit down and write out my good points and character strengths as well as my weaknesses and shortcomings.

When I was fifteen, in ninth grade, I went with my class to Israel on a summer learning/touring program. Our base was a youth hostel in Moshav Beit Meir, seventeen kilometers outside of Jerusalem. The *moshav* (settlement) had many nature trails and parks and an incredibly moving view of the Judean hills surrounding Jerusalem.

One Friday night, we welcomed the Shabbat by singing the mystical song to the Shabbat, *Lechah Dodi*, with particular gusto. Even though most of us were traditional and not religious in our observance, for some reason we were all "into it" that night as we watched the red sun set quickly to the sound of "Come O' Bride…the *Shabbat* Queen."

I stopped to listen to the singing for a moment, and heard, or thought I heard, something like four hundred voices instead of the forty voices actually singing. When I stopped to listen I was transfixed—the song, the voices, the setting sun—I was deeply moved and said to myself: Can there be something to all this Judaism "stuff?" It feels as if there is something going on here, something spiritual, which I can't put my finger on or explain. Perhaps it was a moment of spiritual self-awareness. I think the reason this beautiful moment happened was because I stopped to listen to the music… and I was able to hear the music of my awakening soul.

A friend of mine finished first at Yale in his major, engineering, and then finished in the top ten of his class in business school. When he went for an interview with a top management firm, the interviewer asked him how it was that he was so consistently successful in his studies. He replied that throughout his years in school, once a week, for twenty-four hours, he would take a complete break from his studies and go down to Cape Cod to play frisbee on the beach. He wouldn't take any books with him. He would just go to rid himself of the week's tensions and pressures, so that he could have a chance to think about life.

The message here is that I need a day off from personal stresses and strains in order to allow myself to take a personal inventory. Some people do it by meditating, taking a drive in the country, or by going to synagogue. But this process of taking personal inventory is more than just rest and relaxation. Once I begin to wind down, I realize that accessing my spiritual center requires active emotional energy.

Change of pace and relaxation allow me to get in touch with my spiritual center, but to activate it I must begin to analyze my strengths and weaknesses. It means asking myself: What do I really want out of life? How can I make a difference in the world? It is a process of reevaluating and prioritizing my values, and, thereafter, my goals. It is an exercise in self-transformation. Since this actually means re-creating my "self," it takes hard work and time. I must be patient. In the end, however, I actually enjoy re-creating myself. It is the most rewarding thing I can do with my life.

In embarking on this process, I must seek out a personal advisor, a close friend, or a spiritual leader who can help me analyze my "self" objectively. I do not seek advice so that I can abdicate responsibility for deciding for myself. After all, it must be *my* process and *my* decision. However, my advisor can help me objectively clarify the issues.

While spending time in this process of self-reflection—which should take place over a number of weeks, months or even years—I must persevere in my present endeavor, job or relationship, without making any changes in my present situation. This "taking of my pulse" is a process that, of necessity, takes place over time. If I come up with some new revelation about my life, I must not respond impulsively. I must carefully work through the issues of my job, relationship or situation. I must communicate with the people involved in order to try to come up with ways to improve my current situation. I must seek out a financial consultant if I have a business problem, or a therapist if I have a relationship problem. Often the challenge is sent to me to work through, modify the way I am doing things, or put more emphasis on a neglected area.

A MYSTICAL PERSPECTIVE

A HARVARD UNIVERSITY study showed that the average couple speak to each other nine minutes a week. "Hi, dear. How was your day? How are the kids? Please pick up some milk on the way home. Any mail? What's on TV tonight? How's your mother? My back is killing me. Good night." Add it up. It's just not enough time to develop mutual understanding and a deepening relationship. Even watching television together, going to the movies, or inline skating do not foster interpersonal communication. People need to talk to each other, and for meaningful communication we need real time, not just a little "quality time."

The antidote to this problem is to take one day off each week to spend as a family, eating together, conversing, walking together, bonding and yes, praying.

A fixed day per week—Saturday—the Shabbat, the Sabbath—for Jews—is the way to reclaim some organized quality time. Ever heard of a "forced savings" plan? Well, this is a forced spiritual savings plan. It is during this reflective quality time that we can engage in repairing relationships, talk about issues, focus on priorities, and think about how we have fared during the past week. The deeper meaning of the Torah's, "Six days you shall work and on the seventh day you shall rest" (Exodus 20:11) is: six days you shall work *on yourself* and on the seventh day you shall reflect on the changes you have implemented in your life since last week. If all we are is a bit more tired, and only a week older, then we still will not have utilized our time or the Shabbat as tools for growth.

The rules of Judaism regarding Shabbat are important, and should be followed to generate a reflective attitude. God wanted to give us a weekly opportunity and framework for spiritual growth, to build the self, the family and the community. All of these are advanced by Shabbat observance. We need quiet personal space within which to get to know ourselves and reorder our priorities. On Shabbat we can withdraw from the outer clamor of life and listen to the inner music of the soul. As it states in Kings I (19:12): *"kol demamah daka*—the still inner voice,"* shall be heard. And in that inner voice, you will find your true self.

The opening words of the classic 18th century volume *Mesilas Yesharim—The Path of the Just,* by Rabbi Moshe Chaim Luzzato, are: A man must clarify that which is his obligation in *his* world.

One of Judaism's primary mystical thinkers, Rabbi Isaac Ben Solomon Luria, known as The Ari, explained that three things makeup a person's world:

1. *Olam*—one's physical world and material needs.
2. *Shanah*—one's time, and what one does with it.
3. *Nefesh*—one's soul, one's attributes and what one con-

tributes to the world.

Every second of every day, we find ourselves in a different configuration of place, time and abilities, and we can constantly change and grow as a result of all our experiences. At every moment, we can actualize our *nefesh* vis-à-vis the particular time and place in which we find ourselves. Each moment, whether or not its potential is actualized, can be lost forever, but we have the opportunity to actualize the potential of every single moment. On Shabbat, we can actually take stock and reflect on the "new" selves we have become over the past week, by becoming aware of our new *olam*—physical space, on this new *shana* (moment in time), with our newly formed *nefesh*—our new selves. In this way, I can use and recognize Shabbat for the gift that it truly is.

12

THE REAL ME

A SPIRITUAL PERSPECTIVE

WHY IS IT THAT, whenever I make a New Year's resolution to change my habits, I seem to fall back into my old ways within months, weeks or even days? The reason is that though my intentions were good and I was inspired by the moment, I never actually implemented a strategy for change. If I am serious about improving myself, then I must outline a serious step-by-step plan for change.

Let's look at an example. If I have a short temper (and who doesn't?), and tend to yell and scream (I'll only admit to raising my voice), or swear (once I said "golly"), or even resort to throwing things across the room (I'll only admit to dropping things accidentally), I certainly won't be able to change my reactions overnight. What I have to do is devise a plan to modify my angry behavior.

1. First, I must stop throwing things. I can still be angry, yell, scream, and, yes, even swear. But for one month I resolve to control myself, such that I will not throw a toaster or anything else at all at anyone!

2. During the second month, after I have mastered the toaster, I resolve to stop swearing. I can still be angry and yell at the top of my lungs. But no throwing and no cursing.

3. After the throwing and the swearing stops, in the third month of the strategy I will begin to work on speaking in an even, controlled tone of voice. I can count to four thousand. Walk the pet armadillo. Take a cold shower. But I've got to watch that tone of voice. First, I will be "heard" better. My change of tone will shock those around me. A change like this can be deafening. Second, it will improve my own sense of self-respect. Just listen to someone else yell at his kids. It's not pretty, and it doesn't even work. In reality it only fosters resentment.

4. The final hurdle—the anger itself. In the fourth month of my action plan, I can begin to deal with the emotion itself. It is time I stopped hiding behind the "I have a short fuse" excuse. I can say to myself: I feel angry right now. I feel like yelling, but I won't. Slowly, I will come to master my emotion of anger and frustration. After all, I don't want to be a slave to my impulses and instincts forever. I want to liberate myself. It takes hard work, but having a plan gives me a methodology to achieve it.

A MYSTICAL PERSPECTIVE

AS I MENTIONED PREVIOUSLY, when Jacob wrestled with the angel, God took his name Jacob, which means "downtrodden," and added the name Yisroel, which means prevailing over powers that oppose you. What was the significance of the additional name? It testified that Jacob had wrestled with the issues that God wanted him to deal with and had prevailed over his previous nature. The ordeals he endured created an additional dimension to his persona called Yisroel. Just as the contractions and pains of birth cause every new baby to be born, Jacob's ordeal gave birth to a new part of himself.

After Jacob received his additional name, he was sometimes still referred to as Jacob. When he lived up to his new name, he was called by that name—Yisroel. When he slipped back into his old personality, he was called Jacob.

We are Jacob/Yisroel's children in every sense. We too sometimes rise to new levels of self, and we sometimes slip back into our old patterns of behavior. We may ask ourselves, who is the real me? The answer is both are. We are all in a state of constant flux. That's human nature. When we expand and grow, we gain a new name, Yisroel—which also means *"yashar-El—directly from God."* When we work to improve ourselves, God himself lends His name to our efforts.

In Hebrew, the word for man is "Adam," which refers to man's source—*adamah*, the ground. Sometimes we are *adam*, tied to the earthiness of our old selves. But if we take out a moment to rearrange the letters of *adam*, then we get the word *meod*, which means "very" or "more." When we struggle with our issues and overcome them, then we become "more" of ourselves; we move into a higher state of ourselves.

We therefore, are always moving up and down the ladder of our own selves. When we change the vowels of the word *"adamah*—soil or earth," we get the word *"adameh*—I will be like"…God. When we climb the ladder of our inner selves—we can re-create ourselves in the image of God.

13

THE NEW AND IMPROVED GENERATION

A SPIRITUAL PERSPECTIVE

TWO SEVENTY-YEAR-OLD men were traveling by plane to Europe from New York. One was traveling with his grandson, and the other was traveling alone. Every fifteen minutes, the grandson would ask his grandfather whether he could bring him a drink, get him a pillow or blanket or assist him in some way. After a few hours of this incredible display of respect and caring, the lone traveler expressed his amazement that his neighbor's grandchild was so caring. His own grandchildren, he asserted, would never be so interested or caring about his welfare. In fact, he lamented that his grandchildren hardly ever visited him.

His neighbor responded: The reason is actually pretty simple. You believe that humans evolved from the apes. Therefore, every new generation is more advanced, sophisticated and intelligent than the previous generation. When your grandson looks at you, he sees you as being more closely related to an ape than he is; so how can he possibly respect you? My family and I, on the other hand, believe that traditional values are built upon a solid, secure foundation and that, while technology may evolve, values do not. Therefore, when my grandson looks at me he sees me as more closely connected to traditions that help guide us to a more fulfilled way of life. Therefore he respects and cares for me.

This is a common assumption. Many people believe that scientific and technological developments make our generation superior to the old fashioned, more primitive ways of our ancestors. However, if I am brutally honest with myself, then I will admit that technological advances have not brought much advancement to the moral and ethical spheres. While some progress has been made in human rights, in racial and sexual equality, and in battling poverty, the 20th century has also witnessed one hundred and twenty million deaths through two brutal World Wars and countless purges by despotic leaders, like Stalin, Hitler and Mao, who had the most sophisticated weaponry at their disposal. Scientific development is still obviously in need of a moral compass.

Modern society has discarded old-fashioned values at the same time that it has picked up the fast-paced life of microwaves and broadband modems. However, I see that I also have tended to confuse technology with values. I find myself thinking that if something is not modern, then it is not good. So I might be tempted to throw away the old VCR for the new DVD, the old 486 for the new Pentium 5. I would be "out of touch" if I used an old cell phone or a slow internet server, so I might automatically come to think that if my marriage isn't working I should throw that out too!

In fact, most people feel that this attitude has been a contributing factor in the rise of the divorce rate from 8% in 1956 to over 50% in 2002. It would seem that people are not willing to work at things any more. It's easier to just go out and buy the new and improved version. So I must begin investing time and effort in working out the issues in my life and my relationships. Instead of blaming someone else, I need to spend some time taking a spiritual inventory. In our "victim-based" society, I may tend to see myself as a victim of circumstances or of the whims of others. But I must begin taking personal responsibility for my character, my actions and my situation, and do everything that is in my power to improve those things through a serious investment of my own time, energy and resources.

A MYSTICAL PERSPECTIVE

THERE IS A DEEPER message in the story of the two older men on the plane. Our beliefs have ramifications and directly impact the way we conduct our lives and relationships. Belief in evolution can make a person feel that the modern generation has all the answers, and that the previous generation is old-fashioned and out of touch. It's hard to respect people when we feel that way about them. Our prejudice against the older generation may be based on the faulty assumption that they have nothing to offer us. We need to realize, though, that, when it comes to values like respecting the sanctity of human life and searching for meaning in life, that not much has changed over the past few millennia. Technological advances address the "what" and "how," but they do not address the values or the "why" of life.

The grandson on the plane who demonstrated devotion and respect for his elderly grandfather felt that his grandfather, was one generation closer to God's revelation of the Ten Commandments to the world—still the greatest moral document of all time.

It is clear that we are a generation of restless and impatient people. We want fast food, quick results, quick fixes and immediate gratification. If we don't get these, we end our marriages and sometimes even our lives. The challenges that God sends us are meant for us to address and to work at. Granted, if we have invested in a serious and long-term effort and have still not been able to improve things, then a change of the status quo might be an option. However, it should not be the first option. Before "throwing in the towel" there must be a sense of personal responsibility in dealing with life's challenges. We give up too easily these days.

Jacob could have easily thrown in the towel after having endured so many tests and ordeals. However, by facing his challenges, Jacob made his unique personal contribution to the world. For example, through Jacob facing his ordeal with his brother, Esau, and having been forced to deceive his father to receive his rightful blessings of the birthright, the world heard these words from Isaac, "The voice is the voice of Jacob, and the hands are the hands of Esau" (Genesis 27:22). This principle teaches us that the "voice"—the power of the "word" and truth, is more powerful than the hand or the sword. This powerful message for the world came about through Jacob facing and working through his challenge.

The Biblical commentator Rashi quotes a story in the

Midrash stating that when Jacob was escaping from Esau after Esau threatened to kill him, Jacob was confronted by Elifaz, Esau's son, who also threatened to kill Jacob (Genesis 29:10). Jacob gave up all his possessions in exchange for his life, and thus enshrined in the Torah forever the sanctity of life over materialism, for all to see. In the first recorded mugging in history, Elifaz effectively said, "Your money or your life." Jacob replied, "Take my money. Give me life." He overcame adversity and taught the world this lesson only by enduring the threat of death by his nephew.

It was through the ordeal of being tempted by the seductive advances of Potiphar's wife that Joseph obtained the title of *Yosef Hatzaddik*—Joseph the Righteous. He resisted the temptation and went to prison, falsely accused but having maintained his principles of morality. He could only have taught us this eternal lesson by having gone through the ordeal.

14

RIGHTS VERSUS OBLIGATIONS

A SPIRITUAL PERSPECTIVE

THE UNITED STATES CONSTITUTION guarantees the "right to life, liberty and the pursuit of happiness." A "right" is defined as a "freedom that others are morally obligated to respect and protect." In a free and democratic society, I do not have inalienable "rights" to do as I please. I can't play music and disturb my neighbors at three A.M., for example. I only have rights if I act in accordance with my social responsibilities. In a sense, therefore, my "rights" have to be deserved or earned by virtue of my acting in accordance with social norms.

When I apply the terminology of "rights" to my perceived "right" to life, I must ask myself whether I earned my "right" to be in this world. Raise your hand if you had anything to do with the decision to bring yourself into the world? Was it your decision to start inching yourself down the birth canal?

The truth is that I don't have a "right" to life. Life was a gift, a freebie, handed to me on a silver platter. Of course, once I have been given the gift of life, I have the right to protection from anyone else who attempts to infringe upon it. However, in terms of my attitude toward life, I would be adopting a more meaningful outlook if I considered my life to be a "gift" rather than a "right."

The way I choose to view this issue has major ramifications on my worldview. If I feel that I have a right to life, then I may begin to feel that everything is coming to me—that I *deserve* a good job, a good home and a good spouse. I live life in a "gimme" mode. Gimme this and gimme that—it's all coming to me. If, however, I feel that life is a gift, then I feel gratitude for everything I have and for every opportunity that comes my way. Consequently, I will enter into a more productive "obligations" mindset.

Instead of complaining why my spouse has not "been there for me," or why he or she has failed to provide for my emotional and physical needs, I can switch into the more productive mindset of trying to discover how I can fulfill my own obligations toward my spouse. Instead of focusing on what my spouse has *not* done for me lately, I can turn the tables on my own thought process and begin focusing on what I can do and what I have done for my spouse lately. When I focus on my obligations and commitments rather than on my rights, then I can rebuild the basic foundations of my relationships.

When I was dating my wife-to-be, I was always careful to look my best, buy the roses and write the little love notes. I was also always forthcoming with praise and compliments. All that was based on, "What I can do for *you*?" It was magical. I focused on my partner's good points, and I made an effort to be there emotionally.

Then—marriage struck! And everything shifted into, "What are you doing for *me*, and what have you done for me, lately?" It's time to bring back the mentality of courtship. I must stop taking my partner for granted. What happened to all the love and romance? Nothing. It is right there under the surface, somewhere between my "rights" and "obligations." It is merely my attitude that is blocking out the old romance. If I refocus on my obligations, the romance will resurface. "Can I make you some tea, dear? Let me take you out for dinner. I'm so sorry that you are having a tough time, dear. I'm right here for you. What's on your mind?"

If I am able to transform my mindset, I may be pleasantly surprised by the response. Newton's Third Law of Physics states that "every action has an equal and opposite reaction." By concentrating on what I can do for others, I will get a lot back in return. If I initiate a positive action, sentiment or communication, it will almost certainly elicit a positive reaction in return. But someone has got to "jump start" the process and it might as well be me.

The act of giving in itself elicits a good, warm feeling of inner serenity and personal satisfaction. Why? It emanates from activating my spiritual center. By giving to others, I develop my spirituality, which thereby leads to personality growth, which in turn gives rise to a feeling of true happiness.

There is a story of a young mother who found it extremely difficult to love, or even like, her eight-year-old daughter, who had seemed to have a mean streak and simply wouldn't listen to her mother. Her mother even found conversing with her daughter to be strained, and she felt tremendous guilt. "How can I not love my own daughter?" she would think to herself.

So, following the advice of a child psychologist, she began a course of "hug therapy." Once a day, even though she did not feel like it, she would hug her child with a forced smile and tell her that she loved her. After a week, the fake smile softened and her arms loosened up as she hugged her daughter. She then began to stroke her hair as she hugged her. After a few weeks of this daily therapy, something amazing happened…her daughter actually hugged her back. She began sharing her thoughts and feelings with her mother. The relationship had been activated.

This is based on the concept that we *don't* act in accordance with the way we feel, rather, we feel and think, in accordance with the way we act. If we act in a positive and loving way we will start feeling that we are in love. Even if you don't feel it, do it anyway. The love will come.

A MYSTICAL PERSPECTIVE

THE TORAH IS FULL of "old-fashioned" commandments. God commanded us to give charity, keep Shabbat, not to steal and not to commit adultery, just to name a few.

All this "obligation" stuff is not politically correct these days. This religious "coercion" doesn't sound too kosher to most people. If you ask me, though, I think that we need to bring back some of those good old "shalts" and "shalt nots." Why? Because God, as Creator and Supervisor of the Universe, expects a certain standard of behavior from us. Instead of looking at it as if God is pushing us around, let's change our perspective to realize that all these commandments mean that God has confidence in us that we can elevate ourselves to His standards. This means that God believes in us.

In the Torah, there are two types of commandments:

1. Between one person and another person (e.g., charity)
2. Between a person and God (e.g., belief in God)

The correlation between these two categories is that when we fulfill person-to-God commandments, we are reminded that there are standards expected of us, and that makes us realize that we have to act properly in our interpersonal relationships as well.

If we seek out Godliness in our spiritual world, we will also be motivated to seek out the Godliness or goodness in our spouses, children and neighbors. We are very good at catching "red-handed" someone close to us doing something wrong. Somehow we think that criticizing people will motivate them to change or improve their behavior.

However, if instead, we focus on the Godliness in those around us, then we will be motivated to look for ways to catch them "red-handed" doing something *good*. It is God who has commanded us to seek good in others. The famous Golden Rule is often only partially quoted. Many will be surprised to learn that the actual Torah verse states:

"Love your neighbor as yourself; I am God" (Leviticus 19:18).

We are commanded to love others and to treat them well *not* because it is moral, good and wholesome. We are commanded to love others because God has commanded it.

We can perform this commandment by complimenting, praising and encouraging others. By offering praise and encouragement, we can bring out the Godliness in them.

If our spouse is upset about something, it is not supportive to say, "Don't worry, it will be all right." Being supportive means validating, acknowledging and empathizing with the feelings of the other person by saying, "It seems like you're having a difficult time. It must be very frustrating for you to…" This technique helps us enter into the mindset of the other person. More importantly, it shows the other person that we identify with and understand their feelings. We don't have to *solve* their problems, but we do want to establish a connection and show that we're there for them.

Being supportive also entails letting the other person know that you're there simply to listen.

15

MEETING DIANA, THE PRINCESS OF WALES

A SPIRITUAL PERSPECTIVE

WHEN I SERVED AS THE RABBI of the New West End Synagogue, I lived in London's West End, in Bayswater, about two hundred yards from Kensington Palace. We often heard the helicopter of Diana, the late Princess of Wales, hovering perilously over our house as she returned to the Palace following an engagement. On November 29, 1996, I went into my local barbershop, Lucas' Hair Salon, to get a haircut. There was a teenager getting his hair cut by Lucas and there was a young woman sitting next to him who looked very much like Diana, the Princess of Wales. I turned to a middle-aged man sitting by the window and whispered,

"Is that the Princess?"

With a shrug of the shoulders, he replied, "I don't know." (It turns out that he was her security guard.)

A young woman ran into the shop and said breathlessly to the Princess, "May I have a photograph with you?"

Diana replied, "I would rather not."

Then I knew for sure that it was the Princess.

I nodded to the Princess as I sat down on the sofa opposite her and she nodded back.

I said, "I am the rabbi of the local synagogue, in St. Petersburgh Place—"

She cut me off in mid-sentence and said: "You mean rabbis can take a half an hour off for a haircut?"

I replied, "It seems that even princesses can take half an hour off for a haircut!"

Amazingly, in a letter to the princess eight months earlier, I had invited the Princess to join us at our synagogue for the following night's cantorial concert, on November 30, 1996, but the Princess wrote back that she was otherwise engaged. I reminded her of this invitation. "But thank you for inviting me," she said.

I said, "Princess, in Hebrew we have a saying, 'chazak v'e-matz—be strong and of good courage.' I wish the Princess well."

I got up to get my hair washed and then realized that the teenager in the barber chair next to the Princess, who was having mousse put in his hair, was none other than Prince William, the future King of England. After my wash, I went to sit down in Lucas' chair, the very barber chair just vacated by Prince William. I thought to myself: I'm sitting in the very same chair as the future King of England! I vowed then that I would never wash those trousers again.

That night was Friday night and, after my wife lit the Shabbat candles, I said the traditional *kiddush* blessings over the wine.

Then I turned to my wife and kids and said,

"You'll never guess who I met today!"

After a few guesses, I told them, "I met the Princess of Wales! In fact I sat in the very same chair as Prince William, the future King of England." After the excitement died down, I said the following to my young children,

"You know something? I am also a king! Not because I am the king of the house and Mommy is the queen of the house. A king is a person who cares for his subjects and provides for their welfare. I, too, am a king and Mommy is a queen, because we look after you children and care for you and encourage you. We perform the same role kings and queens do for their subjects."

❧ ❧ ❧

I have the capacity to be a king or a queen. However, I often sell myself short. As the popular song by the rock group Kansas goes: "All we are is dust in the wind." No wonder so many people are walking around with a negative self-image. I have to begin relearning my basic worth and value. By showing care and concern for a spouse, child, neighbor or stranger, I can overcome my personal isolation and alienation. I can activate feelings of a positive self-image by developing my giving qualities and by being there for someone.

If I am feeling down, I have the power to take myself out of my negative mindset by reminding myself of my essential royal nature. There is a regal core lying dormant within my being and all I need do is to activate it by doing one act of giving or kindness—for that is the essence of royalty.

No one else can really pull me out of my depression except me. Armed with this new self-knowledge of my regal essence, I now feel empowered to take control of my own life. I need not blame others for my predicament and abdicate responsibility for my state of mind. I am in control and I can talk myself out of my feelings of alienation and isolation by "digging deep" into my spiritual center and getting in touch with my royal, giving and spiritual core. When I act upon this realization, I can actualize this empowered feeling. I can get myself out of the house and visit someone who is less fortunate than me, deliver a meal to an elderly person or volunteer at the local hospital. Then I will be allowing my royal nature to develop and I can look at myself with self-respect and begin to feel positive about my "self."

A MYSTICAL PERSPECTIVE

The essence of royalty or kingship is that the monarch "provides" for and gives to his or her subjects. God, as King, provides us with everything—eyesight, food, oxygen and brainpower, and so on with which we can journey through life. In return, we are obligated to feel and express gratitude to God.

If we were to make a list of the ten things with which we could not possibly live without—isn't it true that most or all of the items on our list have been given to us by a Higher Authority? Go on. Write your list. I'll wait. Isn't it true that this list is comprised of things that you did not create yourself rather that came from beyond you.

Now, the next step in the gratitude process is to enter into a dialogue with God.

Us: "Why have You given me all of these wonderful things, God?"

God: "Because I love you."

Us: "You have time to think about and provide for tiny, insignificant me?"

God: "You are very significant to me because I created you."

Us: "What do You want in return?"

God: "Just say, 'thank you.'"

Us: "Thank You."

℞ ℞ ℞

Gratitude is the basic building block of any relationship. True, it implies that we are indebted to someone for giving to us. However, in that acknowledgment of indebtedness, a bond—known as a relationship—is created. And God wants a relationship with each of us.

There is a story told of a Chassidic rabbi who was about to blow the *shofar* (a ram's horn) on Rosh Hashanah, the Jewish New Year. Everyone in the synagogue readied himself and herself for this solemn moment, for the sounds of the *shofar* to act as a spiritual alarm clock to wake us up and inspire us to get our act together and to become more active in our spiritual lives.

The rabbi stepped forward, and put the *shofar* to his lips... then stepped back. He did not sound the *shofar*. He tried again. He stepped forward and put the *shofar* to his lips. The people leaned closer in anticipation... but the rabbi stepped back again. He tried one more time but simply could not bring himself to conduct the ceremony.

"I cannot blow the *shofar* until our good friend Jacob comes forward and tells us his story."

Jacob, a six-foot-five, twenty-two-year-old, rabbinical student, stepped forward awkwardly.

"Jacob," said the Rabbi, "you recently got married to Hannah, is that right?"

"Yes, Rabbi," answered Jacob shyly.

"I cannot blow the *shofar* on this holy day until you tell us a very important thing. Tell us, when you speak to your new wife, Hannah, how do you speak to her?"

"Well," said Jacob, "I am six-feet-five inches tall and my dear wife Hannah is four-feet-eleven inches tall. When I speak to Hannah I have to bend down to speak to her."

"Don't leave out the most important part," pleaded the rabbi. "If you don't tell us what Hannah does when you bend down to speak to her, then I cannot proceed to blow the *shofar*."

The people of the congregation strained and moved closer to hear Jacob's words. He said: "Since I am so tall and Hannah is so short, when I bend down to speak to Hannah, she stands on her tiptoes to speak to me."

"That's it!" cried the Rabbi with delight. "Now I can blow the *shofar*. When I stepped forward to blow the ram's horn, I thought to myself… God is so tall. And like Hannah, I am so small. I couldn't imagine that God, Who is so big and mighty and omniscient, could possibly care about my small insignificant act of blowing the *shofar*. Could He actually care about my tiny deeds? And so I could not bring myself to blow the *shofar*. But then I heard Jacob say that even though he is so tall when he bends down to speak to Hannah, Hannah stands on her tiptoes to speak to Jacob. She may not reach Jacob's full height, but since she tries and he bends to hear, they connect."

The rabbi explained, "God is six-foot-five and we are four-feet-eleven. He bends down and is interested in what we do. We are significant to Him. We cannot reach all the way to God because He is so Great. But all He asks of us is to make an effort. We have to stand on our tiptoes and try to reach Him. If we try to reach up to Him, He will bend down to listen to what we have to say. When I realized this, I decided that I could 'stand on my tiptoes' by blowing the *shofar*."

The first step in our relationship with God, then, is to recognize and to acknowledge that God, as King, cares about our actions, deeds, words and even our thoughts. He is the Royal Provider. The next step in the process is to recognize the royalty within us—within you and me. How? By acting like a king. If we act in a kinglike fashion by providing, caring for, encouraging, in effect "being there" for our spouse, kids, parents, neighbors, friends and community, then we will be acting like God, in His capacity as king or provider.

It is not enough to have relationships. We must nurture and grow these relationships. As we think of ways to act towards those around us with a giving nature, then not only will we be developing our character and growing as a person, but we will also become more like God. And, by emulating and acting like God, we will also be developing our relationship with God. Our relationship with God is so important that it's mentioned in the Ten Commandments.

The Ten Commandments are divided into two tablets or sections. The first five are:

1. *I am the Lord your God*
2. *Have no other gods before Me*
3. *Do not take God's name in vain*
4. *Observe Shabbat*
5. *Honor your parents*

These first five commandments all deal with the relationship between us and God. When we adhere to these obligations, we come to understand that there are standards expected of us by God. By making these demands upon us, God shows us that He believes that we can raise ourselves up to His standards. It is inspiring to realize that God has such confidence in us that He knows that we can achieve a certain level of behavior.

With these first five commandments, God empowers us to act properly and with dignity. Once we are elevated to God's expectations, then it is a small step to begin performing the next five commandments, which deal with the relationship between one person and another person, namely:

6. *Do not murder*

7. *Do not commit adultery*

8. *Do not steal*

9. *Do not bear false witness*

10. *Do not be jealous of your neighbor's possessions*

When we have a relationship with God, we realize that it is not merely out of social convention and fear of the breakdown of society that we refrain from stealing and murdering. It is because God expects this standard of behavior in our interpersonal relationships as well.

Allow me to prove to you, based on the insights of the Maharal of Prague*, that God always intended for our relationships with Him to lead to a proper standard of behavior in our relationships with others. If we line up the Ten Commandments in the two sections of the tablets side by side, then we can see that there is a correlation or underlying theme that connects the

---

* Rabbi Judah Loew, a seminal 16th century Jewish thinker.

commandments that are found opposite each other.

1. I am the Lord your God—6. Do not murder

The underlying theme that connects these two commandments is that if we are able to see the "I am God" or the Godliness in other people then we will never come to murder anyone, or even hurt them physically or emotionally. This includes not putting them down and not speaking badly about them to others. If we look for the godliness or goodliness in the next person then we will be motivated to relate to him or her in a positive fashion.

2. Have no other gods before Me.—7. Do not commit adultery

If we act with faithfulness and loyalty to our spouses, which, these days, is no easy task, then we will learn to relate with loyalty to God. Under the *chuppah*, the wedding canopy, each of us pledges loyalty to our soul mate. At that moment we could never imagine being unfaithful. But there is a big jump between theoretical emotion and practical day-to-day temptations.

It is amazing how one moment of immediate physical gratification can be allowed to destroy a lifetime of loyalty and bonding. The more we work on our loyalty to our spouses the better we will be able to maintain our faith in God, even when He challenges us with things that we feel we do not deserve. Believing in faith is one thing. Living our faith and putting our faith into practice is much harder—but it's very rewarding.

3. Do not take God's name in vain—8. Do not steal

Swearing in the name of God is an attempt to steal God's name from His rightful place and to ascribe Godliness somewhere it just doesn't belong. Even the everyday swearing and cursing that is so prevalent today, even amongst small children, is taking the God-given power of speech and God's name in vain.

When we belittle ourselves through this type of speech, we are lowering the Godliness in ourselves. This is not a matter of being prudish. It is a matter of maintaining our own dignity and bearing. If we swear at every careless driver, then we are introducing a hostile and unhealthy attitude into our personal environments.

4. Observe Shabbat—9. Do not bear false witness

When we look at the wonders of nature and the amazing order that there is in life, we are reminded that we did not create "all this." We were created and we are not the Creator. True, we are creative, but we are only using the raw materials—brain power and silicon—to create and develop the world. We make things from preexisting things—something from something.

God, however, makes the raw materials themselves; something from nothing. Therefore, He requires us to remember this on a weekly basis by observing Shabbat as the day that He created the universe.

If we rest our creative abilities on Shabbat then we are acknowledging God as the Source of our creative abilities. Therefore, we do not turn on the lights from Friday night at sundown until Saturday at nightfall because turning on a light "creates" a circuit and in order to act as a witness to God's Creation of the universe we do not perform acts of creativity that show our mastery over the universe on Shabbat. Hence, those who observe Shabbat witness and give testimony to God as the Creator.

5. Honor your parents—
10. Do not be jealous of your neighbor's possessions

Everything we have, including our talents, abilities, color of our hair and our socio-economic condition come from a combination of our genes and our immediate environment. Of course we can develop what our parents have bequeathed to us by heredity. Thus, whatever we have has been hand picked for us by a higher authority, namely, by God.

Being jealous of our neighbor's spouse, Jaguar or new swimming pool is to deny that God has basically hand picked our abilities and socio-economic class to meet our particular challenges. What our neighbor has was hand picked for him to meet his needs and challenges. Therefore, we do not have to be jealous of our neighbors. We need only to concentrate on our own challenges and develop our skills, abilities and financial status. (Well, don't just stand there take a course!). But being jealous is a waste of energy that can be better exerted on developing ourselves.

16

SELF-ESTEEM

A SPIRITUAL PERSPECTIVE

HAVE YOU EVER WONDERED how the Japanese Bonsai tree stays so perfectly small? Does the botanist clip the new sprouts every day with a tiny pair of scissors? Guess again. The secret lies in trimming the roots of the Bonsai tree. The crown of the tree matches the root system. Long roots give you a wide crown of branches. Short roots lead to short branches.

Just like roots are crucial to a tree's growth, so too the root of *my* spiritual center is my self-esteem. If I see myself as a person of value and worth, then this will be reflected in my mindset and attitude. I will be able to approach any challenge with a positive "yes, I can" attitude.

How do I acquire a positive self-image if I have carried a negative self image with me for years? I was never quite good enough in the eyes of my parents, I never achieved that "potential" that my teachers wrote about in my school report cards, my friends really never included me in the "with it" or "in" crowd. How am I going to transform many years of knocks and blows to my self-concept into a self-respecting one?

Let's delve deeper into our spiritual center to see if we can activate our self-esteem. In a moment of introspection, write down on a piece of paper the ways which, during your childhood and teenage years people "put you down."

Now, let's do a relaxation exercise. Sitting in a comfortable chair or lying on a bed, relax by sending your mind into your toes—now relax the muscles in your toes by massaging them from the "inside" with your mind. Your toes should begin to feel light and tingle. This should take about thirty to forty-five seconds. Now move your mind up to your shins and massage your shin muscles in the same way. Now move to your knees, then your thighs, your abdomen, stomach, neck, shoulders, temples and eyes. This should take a further two minutes.

Relax, now take yourself back to the age you were when a particular person "put you down" and imagine that person standing in front of you. Go to that place, the age you were then…be "there." Now, tell that person what you always wanted to say but never had the opportunity. Try to do it in a calm and even tone. Go on—have a conversation. Say what you always wanted to say but never did. Speak to the individual and set the situation straight.

What would he say in response to you? Say it out loud. Respond to him or her again. By engaging in this "conversation" you will be reliving the experience and you will be able to fix up the emotional pain retroactively. Now, on the count of five, slowly come back to the present. Open your eyes. You have now initiated the process of healing.

Let me share with you a self-esteem exercise which is outlined in detail by Dr. Nathaniel Branden in his book, *How to Improve Your Self-Esteem* (Bantam Books, New York, 1987). While you are in this "earlier age consciousness," become aware that those "put down" experiences may have become incorporated into your developing identity and self-concept. By doing so you can get in touch with those negative feelings. You feel the vulnerable child within you.

Now, come back to your adult self and reach out and give that earlier child or teenager—which is you—only younger, a warm hug. Tell the child or teenager within you that it will be okay. Make friends with the child or teenager in yourself. Embrace the child or teenager as you would care for your own child. Begin to accept that child or teenager as being an earlier version of yourself.

Accepting or coming to terms with yourself, and realizing that you have intrinsic worth and value, are prerequisites for reprogramming yourself with basic self-esteem. Now, your root system can once again extend into the soil or foundation of your psyche and begin to anchor your identity and self-concept.

❧ ❧ ❧

Now that we discussed the importance of a tree's roots, a second aspect of a tree is its species or type. There are many trees, including for example, eucalyptus, birch and oak trees. As with different types of trees so, too, there are different personality types; outgoing, warm, shy and generous, etc. If the spine or trunk of the tree gives a tree its strength, what is my strength?

What do I stand for? What are my values?

Sometimes even at a person's death it's unclear to relatives what the deceased stood for, what their values were. When the unfortunate happens and I have to conduct a funeral I ask the family what they would like me to include in the eulogy. I ask the next of kin to describe the deceased for me and to tell me his or her values.

"What was the theme of his life?" I will ask. "What did she stand for? What is the most important idea or message that he taught you about life? How is the world a better place now because of her life?"

Often the family members give me a puzzled look. "Well," said one, "My mother loved to play bridge and loved the theatre."

"That is helpful," I would say, "but is that what you want me to use in the eulogy? Bridge and theatre?"

"What do you mean by 'theme' of her life?" they will ask.

In order to drive the point home I would usually have to say, "What was he or she willing to die for?" Now, that's a tough question, rabbi. Is it though?

Isn't that the question that we should be asking ourselves during our lifetime, rather than only at the end? What contribution am I making to my family, community and ultimately to society? What makes me unique? In essence, what is the special mission that I was put into this world to accomplish?

Each person has a special contribution or addition to make to society. Not everyone can discover the vaccine for polio or cure cancer. What, however, is my unique mission or responsibility within my corner of the world? I can and do have an important influence and I do affect the lives of the members of my family, friends and community. My actions have a ripple effect on others. I should not underestimate the significant affect I can and do have on those around me.

In order to figure out what I am doing here, I have to take an inventory of my good qualities and strengths. Write them down. They could include qualities like: caring, compassionate, courageous, friendly and resilient. Based on an honest appraisal of my strengths and set in the context of my personal circumstances, I can begin analyzing what contribution I am expected to make. How can I use my talents and abilities to change my community for the better? How can I make my life count?

Each of us must constantly take stock of our abilities and ask ourselves: am I making the highest and best use of my personality, both in my personal, family, and community life and in my professional, and business life. Once I am aware of the contribution I can make, then I can begin to become aware that not only do I have value and intrinsic worth just because I "am" but that I am also "competent." I am a capable individual who can make a difference in the lives of others. This is what is called "making a name for oneself" in the world. This awareness—that I am a capable and competent individual—is the second component of self-esteem.

かか か

The third part of a tree is its crown, comprising its branches, leaves, blossoms and fruit.

This is the dynamic part of the tree that visibly changes from season to season. The crown of the individual represents a person's deeds or actions. The root system, the core of my self-esteem, establishes my value by virtue of just "being" rather than doing or accomplishing. I have worth because I am part of the world and I am a player on the stage of life. I am okay merely because I am here.

Appreciating just "being" and being aware of my independent self-value is the root of my "tree" of life. Secondly, I have a trunk—which means that I have a name by which others identify me by. Being aware that I am a capable individual and that I am competent to provide my unique contribution is symbolized by the type of tree I am that makes up a part of the garden or forest.

The third, or crowning part of my self-esteem is actually getting out there and doing whatever I've decided is my contribution. This is the action part of the self. The part of the tree that is seen by others to be growing or moving are the branches, leaves and fruit—the symbol of the applied self. I am going to apply my self-concept and actualize my potential through pro-actively contributing meaningfully to my relationships, my workplace and my community. So here you can see a complete model of the roots, trunk and branches of the self-esteem tree.

♈ ♈ ♈

Just before a child learns to crawl forwards, the child can often be seen crawling backwards. "Hey kiddo, you're going the wrong way." Just before the child learns to walk, there is often a frustrating period as the child wants to achieve something new but just doesn't quite have the ability to actualize his or her desire to get from point A to point B. Then, suddenly there is a breakthrough-a burst of steps—a flurry of activity to leave the security of the couch and to venture out "where no baby has gone before."

This model can be applied to personal growth. Immediately

before a graduation to the next level of personality growth there is often a period of introspection, reflection, even frustration. I may be stuck on a certain issue or personality trait or attribute which I would like to graduate from or change. I know where I want to get to, but I just can't imagine getting over this hurdle. Sometimes it is even comforting to stay at my current level because I know it and I can get away with functioning at a level short of my potential. After all, greater growth leads to more responsibility. This kind of thinking often leaves one confused, frustrated and in a state of inner turmoil.

The same model can be found in nature. Immediately before the renewing rains of spring there is a blustery, snow-swept winter. Nothing grows. The wind cuts through my coat. I wonder when "all this" is going to end. It is a time of introspection and inner reflection. I contemplate the coming thaw. It is a frustrating time, but it need not be.

If I "make friends" with the wintry period of my life and accept that this is a "down" time, then I need not fight it. Just like nature needs a time of dormant reflection, so do I. I can remind myself that without winter there can be no spring. Then I can put the "low" period of my spiritual metabolism into the perspective of all the seasons. Hang in there, spring is coming. The springtime of my spiritual being is also coming.

This is where my character growth comes into play. The winter was necessary to cause me to reflect upon my life and where it is going. It is necessary that I take a breather and get a perspective on my life and my priorities, just as an artist steps back from his canvas to evaluate the dimensions of his painting. Similarly, I can use the wintry period to step back and take stock of my strengths and weaknesses and "where I can go grow from here."

A MYSTICAL PERSPECTIVE

RABBI ABRAHAM TWERSKI, M.D., a renowned psychiatrist, and founder of the Gateway Rehabilitation Clinic for substance and alcohol addiction in Pittsburgh, in his book, *I am I* (Shaar Press, New York), writes that the ultimate way to gain self-esteem is to become aware of the source of my "self" which will in turn instill in me esteem or worth. This is Step One of the twelve steps of Alcoholics Anonymous which states:

I give myself over to a higher Power.

Having self-esteem means that we have an awareness that our lives have intrinsic value. We have worth because a Higher Power—God—created us and planted within us a sanctity or specialness. As the Torah states, "…and God blew into the nostrils of man the breath of living spirit…" (Genesis 2:7).

The living spirit within us is our life force which has been given to us by God. Our "self" is made up of our "horse" or body. Our sense of self "esteem" is conceptualized in our spiritual center—our souls. "Self-esteem" is the value that we have as a combination of our bodies and souls which together make up our sense of self—our identities, our psyches and our personalities.

Our global self-esteem is based on our various self-concepts:

1. Physical self-concept: our perceptions of our own physical appearance and health;

2. Spiritual self-concept: our perceptions of ourselves as "good" or "bad" people, our relationship to God and satisfaction with our religious feelings;

3. Personal self-concept: our perceptions of our personality, our sense of adequacy as individuals separate and distinct from

our relationships to others;

4. Family self-concept: our perceptions of our sense of adequacy, worth and value as a family member;

5. Social self-concept: our perceptions of our sense of adequacy in our social interactions.

All of these frames of reference create in our minds a vision of our "selves"—our self-image—which leads to an evaluation of our level of self-acceptance. If we accept and value ourselves, in all of our "self-concepts," then we will have healthy global self-esteem.

If we are aware of the fact that God has endowed us with self-esteem then we can allow ourselves to appreciate that we are people with God-given sanctity—that we each have intrinsic value. The very fact that we are alive and aware of our inner spirit or spiritual center gives us this sense of worth. We are of value just by being. What we do with our life energy and how we translate our psyches into life's situations and challenges is up to our "choosing center" that is located in our souls.

God challenges us with hurdles and crises in order to push us to develop our abilities and our competence in dealing with life's situations. It is precisely as a result of these challenges that we are propelled into pursuing our private and public missions.

Friday night is an extraordinarily spiritual, mystical and transcendent evening. The Shabbat candles, chanting the *Lecha Dodi* prayer, walking home with our kids, singing *Shalom Aleichem*, husband's praising their wives with King Solomon's famous verses of Proverbs the—*Aishes Chayil*—it's all intensely moving and uplifting. And then it's time to bless the children before *Kiddush*. The problem is: Who are we that we are worthy to "bless" our children? If they only knew what we were really about…. The Rashbam*, says that we bless our children just as the *kohanim* (the priests) bless us, "*Ko sivarchu es Bnei Yisroel*—so shall you bless the children of Israel" (Numbers 6:23).

This is the special moment when we place our hands on our daughters' heads and say: *May God make you like Sarah, Rebecca, Rachel and Leah.* And for our sons we say, *May God make you like Efraim and Menashe.*

These are our personal prayers to God that He Bless our children. We are not ascending to the Heavens when we bless our kids—we are asking God to *descend* from the heavens and into our lives. We nurture, guide and educate these kids to the best of our abilities—and so we are entitled to ask for God's help and guidance. After all, God chose us to look after and mold these *neshamos* (souls)—so aren't we worthy of asking for His blessing? If He believes that each one of us can do this crucial life-giving and life-molding job—then shouldn't *we* think that we are entitled and entrusted with all that is necessary for us to achieve this God-given task? God believes we can—so therefore we also have to start believing in ourselves. We are up to the job!

Our job is to establish a warm, emotional connection with our children at this moment of the Friday night blessings. We should hold our children affectionately and sing the blessings. Whisper a special secret to them. Make them feel holy. Let them know that God loves them, and that you do too.

---

* A 12th century Biblical commentator, the grandson of Rashi.

17

LIKE YOURSELF

WHILE TEACHING A CLASS in philosophy, I asked my students whether they thought they actually existed. Two students argued that they did not really exist and that they were merely dreaming that they were alive. I said that it was a bit farfetched to believe that we were all dreaming the same dream at the same time.

Sometimes a person will go to great lengths to pretend that he is not alive and thereby avoid having to face reality. I see, feel, hear and smell—I sense and I interact with others. I experience the presence of others and in turn they recognize the reality of our existence. Otherwise, who is that fellow talking to? To me.

On a deeper level I "know" in my spiritual center that I am alive. This self-awareness of "being" can lead to the realization that I am human, a part of the world and thereby have intrinsic worth and value. This is the basic ingredient and prerequisite of acquiring self-esteem—an awareness that I am alive in the here and now. I am a personality and I have an identity. I must now learn to face and enjoy the reality of my being here.

That initial realization is only Step One of the process. Step Two would be to begin to like my "self." I have good character traits and values which make me a "good" person. Sure, there are some things about myself I may not be too pleased with, but I do have an innate, good nature which more than outweighs my shortcomings.

If I am to learn to like myself, I have to work on developing this inner goodness by performing acts of goodness and kindness. Sure it takes effort and may involve setting aside my own wants and desires for the benefit of my spouse, kids, parents, co-workers and neighbors. I will begin to like myself more and this will help further develop my self-esteem.

Learning to like yourself is no easy task, especially if you have a history of low self-esteem. Learning to like the person you are takes work. If this sounds like you, then it's best to start with the admission that you don't have self-esteem. This feeling may have been with you for as long as you remember. The reason for this self-perception is that your identity may have been formed by negative feedback from significant others, i.e., from parents, teachers or peers which you applied to your sense of self.

You came to believe that your "bad" behavior meant that you were a bad person (but after all, many of us were a little *chutzpadik*—willful—when we were kids). This negative perception of yourself was unwarranted. It was simply unfounded. You may feel inadequate and inferior—but it is based on an erroneous thinking process. In order to start liking yourself, you have to correct those mistaken assumptions about yourself.

A good program for self-esteem enhancement was developed by Rabbi Abraham J. Twerski, M.D. and can be found on the Internet at www.12steps2selfesteem.com.

A MYSTICAL PERSPECTIVE

THE PURPOSE OF LIFE is to become as much as possible like God or the *Ein Sof*. We can do this by working on ourselves in terms of character growth. The *Ein Sof* is infinite, all knowing, perfectly patient and a terrific listener. So too, our job is to work toward our infinite growth by becoming more knowledgeable, more patient with our spouses, kids and our selves, and to become better listeners. Getting to know God is a little bit like getting to know a favorite author. The more we read about an author the more we come to know his mind and the way he thinks about the world.

Similarly, the more we contemplate and study the attributes of the *Ein Sof* through the study of the Torah—as it expresses God's will and intent—the more we will be able to know the standard that God expects us to strive towards. In fact, the prophet Jeremiah elucidates this particular point when he says,

"But let him that glorifies God, glory in this, that he understands and knows me, that I am the Lord who exercises lovingkindness, judgment and righteousness, in the earth for in these things I delight, says the Lord" (Jeremiah 9:23).

A Spanish medieval Torah commentator, Abraham Ibn Ezra, explains this verse as follows: One cannot know God unless one knows one's own self—body and soul, for anyone who does not know his own makeup and abilities—what knowledge can he attain of God?

In order to get to know the *Ein Sof* one has to gain a sense of self-awareness through introspection and self evaluation. Life's challenges are meant to teach us lessons about our "selves"—where we are strong and where we are weak and what strengths and weaknesses we should concentrate and improve upon. Our sense of self has to be pushed and stretched, otherwise it will tend to take a break and remain in a state of inertia, and this would cause us to miss the point of our existence.

18

THE DEVIL MADE
ME DO IT

A SPIRITUAL PERSPECTIVE

"I'M ONLY HUMAN, after all," is the usual excuse. "I was under pressure, you know," is another. "I have always said that I'm no saint..." is not bad. I couldn't help myself—you would have done the same!" is non-remorseful. "I could not resist the temptation," is the most honest.

Yes, I can come up with many creative excuses to explain my failings and mistakes, but it is important to remember that, while the mistake was a failing, I was not and am not a failure. Understanding this distinction will keep my self-esteem intact while allowing me to improve my behavior in a healthy way.

But let's get to the real issue. How many times could I have actually resisted that temptation, rather than giving in? If I use the "I'm no saint" or "you would have done the same" excuse then there's nothing to talk about. However, if there is a sense of regret or remorse, or if I am upset with myself for having given in, then let's find out how I can "win" the next time.

The good angel, the floppy, white thing on my shoulder, argues for personal growth. "You can do it," he says. "You know how good it will feel to win this battle. You'll grow as a person and thereby develop your true self."

The little red guy with the pointy ears, wry laugh and a pitchfork on your left shoulder says: "Give me a break! Get a life! That guy is a 'no-goodnik,' and you know it. Give him what he deserves! Right between the eyes. Don't be a *shmatta* (rag); don't let him walk all over you. Take a stand for your rights. Live a little! Go for it!"

Now who do you believe—who do you listen to? They both are making valid points. Don't turn to me on this one, this is your decision!

I guess it comes down to delaying immediate gratification. A hungry lion can't say, "I'll give that cute little antelope a break today. He's only six months old—and the baby of the family. I ate two days ago, another day is *nisht geferlach* (no big deal)…"

The difference between myself and the lion, is that while the lion acts on impulse, I can at least choose to act with *conscience*. And sometimes I do. I can delay the immediate gratification of my body for the spiritual pleasure that self-control and self-mastery brings.

I guess it comes down to a battle between the two aspects or spheres of influence of my life—my physical side versus my spiritual side. It depends on what I want out of life and on which plane I choose to live. Will I respond from my emotional self, which is driven by my heart, or will I respond from my intellectual and rational self, which is driven by my mind, and which keeps my emotions in check. Realizing that the choice is mine may feel scary, but it is also astonishingly empowering.

A MYSTICAL PERSPECTIVE

THE SOURCE OF ANY and all of the mistakes we might make today can be found in the three aspects of sin, namely, desire, jealousy, and honor. You can see these three aspects of sin when Adam and Eve committed the sin of eating from the fruit of the *Etz Hada'as*—the Tree of Knowledge of good and evil.

Regarding desire, the Torah informs us about Eve: "It was desirous in her eyes" (Genesis 3:6). Lust. Impulse. That new Jaguar, that cheeseburger, that dress, that apple…the desire may be too much for me to resist…I have to have it—it is desirable in my eyes.

In reference to jealousy, the account in the Torah goes on to say: "And she gave to her husband with her and he ate" (Genesis 3:6). Why did the Torah have to add the words: "with her." Don't we know that if Eve was talking to Adam that he was "with her?" Rashi explains that these extra words express Eve's jealousy of her husband's freedom. "If I eat alone and he does not, then I will be punished and he will be free to marry someone else," reasoned Eve. So Eve wanted Adam to be "with her" at his expense in her mistake of eating from the tree of knowledge of good and evil. Similarly, our jealousy toward our neighbor's new car, new house, or their spouse…may lead us to seek those things for ourselves—that are either at their expense or at the expense of other more important things in our lives.

Finally, the snake said: "And you will be like God" (Genesis 3:5). The snake, which is the same thing as the little red guy with the pitchfork on my shoulder, tempted Eve with pride and honor—to be like God. I want my name on the plaque, I want to sit at the head table, there are principles, you know…and are all sourced in this mistake—the pursuit of honor.

This first couple—in their first disobedience to the first command by God—has to be the source of any and all mistakes that you and I might make, today. The issues that Adam and Eve faced are the same dilemmas we face—only the surroundings are changed. Adam and Eve—are really you and I. Maybe we should read the Garden of Eden "story" again—and then maybe we can begin to uncover even more secrets of human nature.

When Adam was asked by God, "Did you eat from the tree from which I commanded you not to eat?" Adam responded to God's challenge by passing the buck: "The woman whom you gave unto me—she gave me and I ate" (Genesis 3:12).

Typical response. When we are first challenged by our spouse, parents or boss, isn't our first inclination to find a scapegoat and blame someone else? Any wonder why? Because Adam—who is you and me—naturally reacts that way. President Harry S. Truman, however, learned Adam's lesson. He had a big sign on his desk which said: The buck stops here. It only took a few thousand years for someone in authority to fix up Adam's mistake. So its merely an out of date, irrelevant, fable—they say, this Garden of Eden story of ours—or is it?

So man moved on to the next generation and, when Cain killed Abel, God challenged Cain and said, "Where is Abel your brother?" And Cain answered: "Am I my brother's keeper?" (Genesis 4:9). At least this next generation improved upon

Adam's response. Adam blamed Eve. But Cain did not blame someone else. He did, however, fail, to take personal responsibility for his actions.

So then God moved to the next stage of mankind and challenged Noah, and told him that there was going to be a flood. Now, finally, there was someone who took responsibility. He built the ark for himself, his wife and his sons and daughters in law. He met God's challenge by doing something for his family. But Noah did not fully develop his sense of responsibility because he failed to go out to the people and cause them to repair their ways. He looked only after his own family and no more. That is why he was known in the Torah as "...a righteous man in his generations" (Genesis 6:9). Rashi comments, "had he lived in Abraham's generation he would not have been considered great."

And so God waited ten more generations until he found a man who had developed into a person who was worthy of becoming the father of the Jewish people—Abraham. When God told Abraham that he was about to destroy Sodom— Abraham entered into the first plea bargain in history—"If You find 50, 45, 40, 35, 30, 20, 10 righteous people will you spare the city?" (Genesis 18:23). Abraham became the first person to achieve his potential—by caring for those people who were outside his family. He became the *ish chesed*—the man who brought the concept and attribute of loving-kindness to the world.

So the stories of Genesis speak to us and they challenge us to grow from an Adam into an Abraham. We are astonished to watch as man develops beyond his capacity for immediate gratification—Adam, into an Abraham, who puts aside his personal needs for others. This is what God wants from us—to forgo the immediate gratification of the body and to develop the self—the soul.

And God tells us how to do this, through the manner in which he admonished Adam. God did not punish Adam. He instructed him how to rectify his behavior and effect a *tikun olam*—the rectification of the world. "By the sweat of your brow you shall eat bread" (Genesis 3:19). Why the brow? Why didn't God say, "By the sweat of your back?" The answer is because the brow—the forehead, represents the seat of the mind—the intellect. As it were, God said: "Instead of your using your intellect to serve me—you used it to serve yourself. Therefore you are now going to have to use your intellect to fight for your daily bread."

The word *lechem* (bread), is also the root of the word *milchamah* (war). Through that word God is saying to us: "You are going to have to fight nature and compete with your fellow man in the marketplace wars. But remember Adam, the earth is cursed because of you—you are going to have to struggle with nature to earn your bread. And also remember one thing—I never said that you, Adam, are cursed. I only said that the land is cursed. You—your decision-making center—your soul—is pure, and untainted. All you have to do to get back on track is to use your intellect to serve God's purposes, rather than your own."

And that is the essence of our choice—who is in control, our body or our soul?—which really in essence means, who is in charge, us or God?

The Jewish view is that we are born good—untainted by Adam's mistake. I say mistake, instead of "sin," because the Hebrew word "*chayt*—sin" comes from the word "*l'hachti*" which, as Rabbi J. B. Soloveitchik*, has pointed out, means "to

---

* A 20th century rabbinic Jewish leader, philosopher, and talmudist (1900-1993).

miss the mark." By eating from the Tree of Knowledge of Good and Evil, against God's will, Adam "missed the mark." *Chayt* does not imply a King James Bible type of sin—that's a mis-translation. Adam was not evil; rather, he simply "missed the mark."

There are consequences in the world due to Adam's mistake, but humans are still considered innately good. We are challenged by temptation, but we are not evil.

The little red man may challenge me and part of my nature—but I am *not* him. He makes representations to my pure decision-making spiritual center—but I do not have to listen. But this *yetzer hara* fellow, this evil inclination guy, has got himself a great PR agent. He gets all the lead stories in the press. He has cornered the market. All we hear is: "I was pressured. I was tempted. I'm no saint…" He has so many ways to say, "you gave in."

So what about the *yetzer hatov*—the good inclination? He is modest and quiet. He hides from the limelight, and has a humble press agent. You never hear, "The *yetzer hatov* wins the day. He resisted temptation and gave more money to charity that he did last year!" No. He never gets the lead stories, because part of the *yetzer hatov* is modesty and humility. He'll never promote himself. So I guess we'll have to!

So what about your *yetzer hatov*—your good inclination? You do have a good inclination, a dimension that wants the soul in you to lead and to develop your self and your character. So use it. Use your intellect, your *sechel* (your mind). Let's not give in so easily. You have a good side, you have a good nature—you are a good person.

The *yetzer hara* will try to convince you that you are a worthless, negative person. It tries to tell you that you have no value.

It tries to get you to say to yourself, "what's the difference, I might as well!" No! Instead use your intellect and activate your self-esteem! You have intrinsic worth because you have God-given intrinsic value. He placed a part of Himself in you. After all, that is what your soul is—a *chelek elokah mimaal*—a piece of God from up above. It is good, pure and eternal.

You can develop the eternal in you—your eternal self—by rising above the *yetzer hara*. In fact, that is why God placed the *yetzer hara* and his arguments before you, so that you can listen and reject his arguments by listening to your intellect and utilizing your *yetzer hatov*. As God said to Cain, "Sin crouches at the door but you can master it" (Genesis 4:7).

This battle between your *yetzer hara* and your *yetzer hatov* is a lifelong process. You will win some and lose some. But you have to keep struggling, because with the struggle there is growth and expansion, which brings you closer to the *Ein Sof*.

19

LONELINESS

THERE IS ONE PREREQUISITE before I can hold myself in esteem and like myself. That is self-awareness. I must develop an awareness of my own identity before I can begin to like my "self." How do I go about becoming more aware of my self?

Let me take you back to your childhood, in fact, let us regress to the time we were toddlers. Remember that time when you were just beginning to take your first steps? You had been holding onto the sofa in the living room and your parents and grandparents were clapping and cheering as you let go of the sofa with one hand and took a step forward. Then you completely let go of the couch and took two or three shaky, but quick steps into the middle of the room. You were smiling, two bottom teeth flashing and everyone was screaming, "You did it! Hooray! You are walking!"

As you took each new step, your father took a step backward as he held out his hands for you to keep walking. (Nice guy, your dad). And then, something happened. You stopped in the middle of the room and realized that you were not holding on to anything or anyone. You were on your own in the middle of the room. "How did I get here?" you asked yourself. "What am I doing out here all by myself without anything to hold me up? I can't do this!" And promptly, you sat down on the floor in a flood of tears and sobs and your mommy rushed over and scooped you up.

Remember that moment? I don't suppose you do. But it did happen. That moment, as you stood in the middle of the room on your own, which was one second before you plopped down, was that crucial first moment of self awareness that you were independent—not intrinsically connected to anyone else. You were no longer holding onto the couch or onto Mommy's apron strings. It was just you and the world. That was the first second you subconsciously realized that you were a person—a "self" in your own right. And what is the natural reaction to this realization of a personal identity? Absolute terror. So you sat down.

This experience and the feeling it engendered within you is ingrained in your psyche. That feeling is one of fear of your own identity—of your "self"—of being alone within your own self. I believe that this is part of the human condition. It is an existential feeling of being alone on your own in the big living room called the world.

This realization can give rise to your feeling alienated, isolated and lonely. It is natural—it is part of the human makeup. Whenever I feel isolated or alienated in life, then I am actually tapping into the same feeling that I first experienced standing alone in the middle of my parents' living room. However, I would like to suggest that these scary, lonely situations that we experience in life do not have to give rise to a feeling of loneliness or personal angst, alienation or personal "exile." All I have to do is use my mind instead of my emotions. I am alone in the world in that only I have my particular personality created from my unique DNA, my upbringing, environment and unique mix of abilities and weaknesses.

Of course I am alone in the world and that's because I am unique! No one else in the universe has my mix of genetic nature and environmental nurturing. I am different and therefore alone. Now, what do I do with this realization? I can say to myself, I am different and: a) therefore, I am lonely or b) therefore I am unique and special. In order to play my unique role in the world I have to be alone. But this does *not* mean that I have to be lonely.

This awareness of my unique "self" can be a downer or it can be an upper. It can make me feel lonely or it can challenge me in the realization that my unique characteristics enable me to perform a unique job that only I can perform. I have been hand picked for my particular life goals and only I can fulfill them. Using this psychologically-correct terminology I can experience self empowerment and, in this way, turn the liability of being "lonely" into the asset of being "alone" and unique in the world. Instead of living in dread of my loneliness, I can revel in my aloneness.

A MYSTICAL PERSPECTIVE

WHY DIDN'T GOD CREATE man and woman simultaneously as two "separate but equal" individuals? Wouldn't that have been more politically correct? Wouldn't that have solved the "equal pay for equal work" problem right from the start? Furthermore, while we're talking "equality" couldn't have God fostered more brotherly love and "peace among men" had He created a whole community of people simultaneously to underline the basic unity of mankind and to send us the message from the outset that we all have to work "together"? Obviously God decided that creating Adam alone, as a singular being, was a more important message to send to the world at the beginning of time. Why?

The Jerusalem Talmud (*Sanhedrin* 4) asks this question and explains that Adam was created alone so that each and every person who is born could relate and identify with Adam's singularity and aloneness and say: I am Adam.

God obviously felt that the original state of humanity was one of unique individuality and so He created Adam alone. This was God's way of telling us that before we can relate to someone else we have to become self aware—we must learn to relate to ourselves.

God is challenging us to become aware of our separate and unique identities and to get to know ourselves so that we can successfully relate to others. What is our private identity exclusive of our public identities?

My public identity is a father, husband, a Canadian, a rabbi and a lawyer, but what is my private identity? Who is this personal "self" that we need to be aware of before we can relate to somebody or something else? Before we belong to a group or organization which serves to "identify" us, God is saying that we first have to belong to and identify with the subject of our "self."

Some of my best "friends" are lonely. God Himself is "lonely," as we say every day in the morning service, "*Ki Hoo levado*...— For He is singular and on His own." This means that He is independent of any control and that He is the source of our free will. God is the "*Ein od milvado*—there is nothing else besides Him."

This means that He is the source of all life, including creative thought, initiative, energy and enthusiasm. He placed within you and me a spark of Himself—a spiritual center, a soul.

If God is singular, then it must follow that He places this attribute of singularity within us as well. That is why our natural existential selves feel "alone" in the world. But, if we take that feeling or thought to a deeper place within ourselves, we will realize that it is okay to be alone in this way. It allows us to get in touch with our unique identity.

Once we become aware of our independent (albeit dependent on God) selves, then we can initiate, create and enthusiastically produce that which we were put here to accomplish. As we say in the Friday night *Kiddush*: "*asher barah Elokim laasos*— which God created—to do" (Genesis 2:4). The "creation," says the *Alshich*, is God's; the "to do" is for us, to complete God's creation by actualizing our potential of being partners with God in His creation.

This is the meaning and the challenge of Hillel's famous saying in the *Ethics of the Fathers*: "If I am not for myself, who will be for me?" (1:4). Far from being a statement promoting the ego, it is really a challenge that I have to get to know who I am and learn to develop a personal self-concept as a prerequisite to activating my potential.

But why does this process of "getting to know my identity" have to come with so much painful soul searching and inner turmoil? You know the feeling. It's a sense of not being on track with your goals, of losing your grip on life, of feeling like your life is going nowhere; it's like having a bad hair day—only this is a bad life day—and its been lasting a few years. Why do I have to experience the angst of exile from my "self" before I can finally "find myself"? The answer is that only by going through this process of personal exile to personal redemption, can you really achieve a sense of inner identity, inner knowledge and ultimately that elusive goal—inner peace.

The source of this idea of going through a personal exile to find oneself lies in our forefather Jacob's struggle with the angel on the night before he was to encounter his brother, Esau. The Torah states, *"Vayvaser Yaakov levado, vayaavek ish imo, ad alos hashachar*—And he remained alone and a man struggled with him until the break of day"* (Genesis 32:25). Who was this enigmatic man with whom Jacob was struggling? According to the Torah commentator, *Kli Yakar**, the man was Jacob's own *yetzer hara*—his negative self.

Ultimately, Jacob—and each and every one of us—are all *b'nei Yaakov*—children of Jacob—and we each must struggle with our inner selves throughout the night and through the struggles of life—in order to make it to dawn and achieve a breakthrough—a new level of self and new found contentment.

At night there is confusion, things are not clear. We struggle with our inner emotions. In fact, if you are at all self aware you can actually feel the inner battle for control of self, raging passionately within you, but you have to be attuned to your inner voice. Of course, getting to your inner core is a scary and difficult

---

*Rabbi Shlomo Ephraim of Lunshitz, *Rosh Yeshiva* (dean of the yeshiva) in Prague in the early 17th century.

process. Feelings of sadness, inner hurt, past pain and current struggles are brought to the surface. And so it is meant to be. No pain—no gain.

Even the Jewish People as a whole are alone, as Bilaam has reminded us: "*Hein am levadad yishkon*—they are a nation that dwells alone" (Numbers 23:9). Perhaps this sums up Jewish history. We have gone it alone against the world, but we were never lonely because God assured us that we have survived in order to fulfill His hand-picked mission for us—to teach the world about God, spirituality, sanctity and morality. This has been an arduous journey these past thirty-three hundred years. No one wanted us, no one accepts us, no country opened their borders to the refugee ship, the St. Louis, nor to many other boats of its kind during the Holocaust. That has been our story—the Jewish people wandering the sea of history with no port of call except for God Himself. It is only in that existential and real aloneness that we can find out who we are as a nation.

Even within our own Jewish community we argue about who we are. Are we a race? A religion? A culture? A history? Or a family. Who is a Jew? What is a Jew? What does being "chosen" mean—and why can't God choose someone else for a change?

Because He just won't. He chose us and that is our destiny—to grapple with our chosenness and to come to terms with our own Jewish national identity. And if the nation is grappling with its self, then clearly, each individual within the nation is going through exactly the same process as the nation itself. So, we come by soul searching honestly. And you thought it was only your mother's guilt trips!

20

LOVE YOUR
NEIGHBOR AS
YOURSELF

A SPIRITUAL PERSPECTIVE

LAST WEEK MY NEIGHBOR, Howard, drove up in a gleaming new Saab Turbo 900 with spoke wheels, a wood interior—in my favorite color—racing green. I walked over to him as he was getting out of his new car and, shaking his hand heartily, I complimented him, "Mazel tov, Howard—congratulations. It's a beautiful car. Drive it well and in good health. I am so happy for you! You deserve it!"

As I walked back to my own driveway and passed my own 1987 beat up, tired, Chevy station wagon, the one with baseball dents and no fender, I said to myself: Why does he deserve a new Saab? After all, I work just as hard as he does! I am a good person and he is...I work longer hours than he does... and I'm working for the community and...Hold it! What about "Love your neighbor as yourself?" How come I feel this way? Why am I so bitter?

I'll have to admit it then…I don't love my neighbor, Howard, as I love myself. If I did I would be as happy for him as I would be for myself…racing green, yet! It had to be racing green! What happened to my sense of brotherly love? Maybe I'm not such a nice guy after all?

And then I figured it out. If I am supposed to love my neighbor *as myself* I can only love him as much as I love *myself*. If I don't love or even like myself then I can hardly love or even like Howard or be happy for his success. If I am not secure in my own abilities and possessions and lot in life then I can't possibly be really happy when my neighbor adds an extension to his house, goes on his third holiday this year and is putting in a sunken, kidney-shaped swimming pool in his backyard—what a weird shape!

So it seems that having a poor self-image has ramifications beyond myself. Perhaps my relationships have suffered because I have persisted in this mode. Maybe it's time I began acting more responsibly towards myself and to others by working on my self-image. It is not easy. It takes effort. It means erasing old ideas about myself and replacing them with a new self-image. It also requires an awareness that I have a self-esteem problem and a willingness and desire to change it.

Some people have the mistaken notion that it is haughty or prideful to believe in yourself. This is absolutely false. Believing in oneself is essential not only for healthy functioning, but for successful relationships as well.

My negative self-image will directly impact my ability to bond with my children, spouse and parents, in a healthy way. If

I often feel attacked or criticized by those closest to me, it might well be that I have been taking their comments the wrong way. The first step is to admit that my "take" on their comments is coming from my poor self-image.

A MYSTICAL PERSPECTIVE

I LIKE HOWARD, REALLY. And I am truly happy that he just bought a new country house in upstate New York, you know, the rustic log cabin type that costs more than the one in the city.

You know how I achieved this change of heart? I read and integrated the words of *Ethics of the Fathers*, "Who is rich? He who is happy with his portion" (4:1). And just how I am supposed to be happy with my beat up Chevy wagon when Howard's driving racing green? By realizing that my portion—my destiny—can be fulfilled with a beat up car. And not just any old beat up car. *My* beat up car. Maybe racing green would "go to my head" and make me focus on the wrong priorities in life. Maybe my values and my communal involvements are more important than possessions. But how do I know that I couldn't fulfill my destiny just as well with racing green and a kidney shape—no, an oval-shaped swimming pool?

The answer lies in the well-known verse in the Torah which states: "Love your neighbor as yourself, I am God" (Leviticus 19:18). Hold it! What's this "I am God" stuff? I never knew that was part of the verse! Well, it is. It's just that we never read the whole verse. It means that I should love my neighbor as myself, because he has "I am God" in him. He has Godliness, goodness and a God given mission to fulfill in the world, just as we do. If we can remember that God gives each of us a particular, unique mission to fulfill and that he also gives each of us the resources necessary to achieve that mission then we can be happy for Howard because he's got what God has decided he needs to fulfill his mission and similarly, we have what we need.

When we add God to the interpersonal equation, the division of possessions is easier to accept. We can learn to accept our abilities and possessions, learn to appreciate our special portion in the world and even begin to like ourselves, because our unique portion enables us to make a unique contribution to the world. Then, and only then, can we start to authentically like our neighbor as ourselves.

21

FEELING SOMEONE ELSE'S PAIN

A SPIRITUAL PERSPECTIVE

I HAVE A CONFESSION TO MAKE. I do experience road rage in traffic jams. Not just any old traffic jam, mind you, a particular type, namely, when there is an accident at the side of the road and all the cars slow down and "rubber neck" in order to get a glimpse of what happened. You quickly understand that there is no other reason for the traffic tie up other than people slowing down to "look." It upsets me because of the *reason* for the delay—that people can't help but gawk at the misfortune of others. "Not true!" the innocent driver will protest. "I slowed down to see if I could help." Sure. If you really wanted to help you would have parked the car, gotten out and done something!

The protesting driver is suggesting that he is doing the honorable thing, namely, slowing down in order to empathize and share someone else's pain. He says that he is identifying with the unfortunate circumstances of the person in the accident by slowing down to show that he cares. What would I have him do, he would ask—drive right past as if nothing happened? Yes! I suggest that, by slowing down to gawk, the driver is not sharing his pain or empathizing. He is merely saying, "I'm glad it's not me."

The authentic way to identify is to translate the feelings of empathy into action. That is genuine identification. Put your money where your mouth is. Talk is cheap. It is not enough to show your sensitivity by saying, "tsk, tsk, isn't that terrible." To share someone's pain, you've got to get down on the floor, hug them and cry with them and see if there is something you can really do to help.

You're never going to believe this, but it's true. I had finished writing the previous paragraph and gone to work. As I was coming home that evening, I was caught in a traffic jam and I noticed a man trying to cross through the heavy traffic on foot. He was, unfortunately, hit by a car just ahead of me, flew ten feet through the air and landed on his side.

As I witnessed this horrible scene, I said to myself, "This has got to be a test to see if I am for real." I pulled off the road, took off my coat and put it under the man's head, which was bleeding. I waited by the man's side until the ambulance arrived to take the injured man to the hospital. I think we ought to be careful about what we say. Someone may actually be listening.

A MYSTICAL PERSPECTIVE

THERE IS A STORY TOLD of a rabbi who called upon a rich

member of his community to solicit funds to buy coal for a poor widow to heat her home in the winter. The rabbi did not actually make the request for the donation until he left the rich man's home and was standing outside saying goodbye in the freezing cold. Halacha—Jewish law—requires a host to escort his or her guest at least six feet outside the door when the guest leaves to give the guest a sense of security and reassurance that the host truly enjoyed the guest's company and is sorry to see him or her leave. The rich man walked the rabbi out the door without bothering to put on his coat thinking that he would be standing on the porch with the rabbi for only a few moments. The rabbi continued small talk with the rich man shivering outside for about six or seven minutes. Then the rabbi asked for the donation.

"Why didn't you ask me while we were in my house?" asked the rich man.

"I wanted you to feel what it meant to be cold, before you responded to my request," said the rabbi.

The host "identified" in a real way with the widow's predicament because he felt what she did. He then donated money to buy coal for all the poor people in the town.

When someone in the Jewish community experiences a bereavement, Jewish law requires that the bereaved stay in their homes for seven days, sit on low chairs to represent their "down" mood and receive callers, who visit to offer comfort and console them. It's called *shiva*—the Hebrew word for seven.

When someone visits the bereaved, Jewish law requires that the visitor sit as far away as possible from the bereaved. The visitor must also refrain from speaking with the bereaved until the bereaved speaks first so as not to disturb the mourner if he or she is lost in thought. The idea of being silent in the presence of the mourner seems a strange requirement. Wouldn't it be better to talk about the weather or current events to take the mourner's mind off his or her loss rather than remain silent? The answer is that to be silent and to thus share the pain with the mourner is the best way of empathizing. We are *not* there to distract the mourner, rather to stay "with" the mourner in his or her pain and to share it.

Being able to share someone else's pain is an indicator and an ingredient of self-esteem. We can only share someone else's pain if we think and feel beyond our own selves. If we feel good about ourselves then we don't need to spend all our time and energy on our "selves," rather we can begin to reach out to others.

The empathy we must feel for others is woven into the daily Jewish prayer service. We Jews never pray for ourselves alone, rather we pray in the plural, i.e., heal us, bless us, hear our voices…The source of this idea comes from the Torah, in Genesis 20:17. Abraham and Sarah, unable to conceive a child, found themselves in a situation where Sarah was abducted by the King Abimelech. God then punished Abimelech and his countrymen with barrenness. Subsequently, Abraham prayed for their recovery and they were healed. The very next verse in the Torah states, "God remembered Sarah and she conceived" (Genesis 21:1).

Rashi comments on this juxtaposition, as follows: "This section, of Sarah conceiving, immediately follows after the section of the recovery of Abimelech's countrymen, to teach us that anyone who requests mercy for his friend, where he himself is in need of the same mercy, he will be answered first." Thus, Sarah conceived before Abimelech's people were healed as a result of Abraham's prayer for them.

A rabbi and teacher of mine related that a woman in his former community in Israel once asked him for a blessing to be able to conceive. He told her that he had no special hotline to God but he suggested that she might pray for his own daughter who had one child many years before and who hadn't been able to conceive since then. She agreed to pray for his daughter and the rabbi asked his own daughter in America to pray for the woman in his own community. A few weeks later he learned that both were expecting, one month apart. His daughter gave birth two months early. The woman in Israel gave birth two weeks late. Each gave birth to a healthy baby girl on the same day. Each had prayed for the other, and each was answered first—which happened to be at the same moment.

22

I DIDN'T KNOW WHETHER TO LAUGH OR CRY

A SPIRITUAL PERSPECTIVE

I FELT SUCH A MIX OF emotions that I didn't know whether to laugh or cry. So I did both. That's it! The way to look at life is to be able to laugh with one eye and cry with the other—at the same time. Life is not all good times and it is not all bad times. I constantly have to "go with the flow" of the ups and downs of everyday life. I might feel that my mood swings are abnormal. They are not. It is my reaction and perspective on them which is the key.

A human being is an amalgam of feelings and emotions. We can feel happiness, fear, hope, frustration, anticipation or anxiety in rapid succession in response to the flow of daily events. This is normal. Yes. You and I are both normal! In fact it is normal to experience overlapping or conflicting emotions. That is what make us human. There is no rule of compartmentalization of feelings. Perspective is the key. I can choose to be "brought down" by these events or I can see them as a symphony with highs and lows. It's all part of the package.

How do I maintain this perspective in the midst of these ups and downs? I can remind myself of my spiritual center. I can use the age-old discipline technique of counting to ten before I react. If I have a problem with my child, for instance, reacting immediately would probably be an instinctive, impulsive and angry reaction, resulting in my screaming at the child, if not spanking him. However, how educationally instructive will that reaction be for the child? How will it teach the child to react to his own frustrating situations? How will it reflect on my own personal growth i.e., my self control? If I think and wait, reflecting and getting in touch with my spiritual choosing center, then I can choose to react calmly, instructively and with educational value. I can choose to respond calmly.

On a good day I've said, "Come here please. I'd like to talk with you. What happened? Did she provoke you? Were you upset or angry? You are entitled to be angry, but you know that it is inappropriate to act upon your anger. You can tell your sister, 'I am angry with you and I would like to hit you,' but you can't." This way the child will learn to get in touch with his or her own choosing center. Then a consequence such as, "Go to your room to think about it," can be seen as a way to reflect and improve, rather than as a punishment.

This "count to one million, before I react" model (I mean "count to ten!") is the technique I can use to switch into my spiritual center in every situation. It can be applied when challenges present themselves in the marital, workplace and child/parent scenarios. If I take my time before I react I will be able to simultaneously "stay with" the situation and stay "real," while at the same time psychologically disconnect from the situation. This will enable me view the situation in perspective and to see the "big picture."

This is basically the concept of cognitive therapy. The theory holds that the way I feel about something and how I experience it depends largely on *my attitude* towards it. The same event will be experienced in extremely different ways by different people.

The problem, however, is that I cannot simply choose which attitude to have. I have a pattern of attitudes which I have learned since childhood which may not be the most desirable or effective way of dealing with certain situations. When faced with a certain challenge I may go into automatic pilot and react the way my parents taught me to react or how I learned to react and cope in my formative years.

The secret is to try to erase the tape of old attitudes by first becoming aware of the way I react to certain situations. I must first observe myself and watch how certain events seem to push certain automatic buttons in me which cause me to react in a certain way. I should watch myself react and say to myself, "Isn't it interesting that I react this way." I should not try to modify my reactions just yet. Once I get a handle on myself and become aware of my patterns, then slowly, as I monitor my reactions, I will be able to unlearn old attitudes and insert more effective reactions into my repertoire.

The second thing I can do when I am in the midst of life's roller coaster ride is to ask myself—which is to ask my spiritual center, what is expected from me here? How can I become a better, more understanding, compassionate, empathic, wise, person through this event or experience. Thus, each event will not incapacitate me or "bring me to my knees." Rather, it will lead to a moment of introspection and then personal growth.

A MYSTICAL PERSPECTIVE

THE WORLD IS MADE UP of a series of dualities: black and white, night and day, evil and good, a photograph and its negative... This model was established by God at the beginning of Creation:

"...And it was evening and it was morning, one day" (Genesis 1:5).

The deeper, mystical meaning of this verse is that evening signifies darkness, difficulty, ordeal and crisis. Morning, with its clarifying dawn, means the ability to see clearly how to deal with, cope or even solve a particular problem. So that's why its good to "sleep on it" and to approach the problem afresh in the morning! The world is made up of both aspects—negatives and positives. Together they make up reality.

I have to learn to hang in there during the night times of my life in order to watch the sunrise. It is precisely to test my faith that these challenges are sent to me in the first place. The test of faith is not to lose my faith. It's easy to give up in the darkest part of the night and throw in the towel. If only I could make it to the morning...

This is the meaning of the verse we say in the psalm for Shabbat, "...to relate Your kindness in the morning and Your faith in the nights" (Psalms 92:3). At night—which means during an ordeal—our faith is tested. In the morning—after we have weathered the ordeal—we see God's kindness.

The Jewish day begins at sundown. God established the world in this way in order to integrate this idea in our souls—that life has its sunsets, and evenings, its trials and dark moments. And yet it also has its dawns and mornings, its joys and its moments of clarity. First we must work through our nights—our challenges—and only when we have worked through these moments of darkness and confusion can we arrive at the clarity that comes with personal growth.

In fact, Jewish history begins this way as well. First comes Ishmael, and only then is there an Isaac. First Esau is born and only then Jacob. First comes the slavery of Egypt, then the redemption of the Exodus. First there is an ordeal, and then there is resolution. Jewish history has always followed this model. We have lived and survived through the ashes, and have enjoyed many redemptions. It happens on both a national and a personal level.

On a personal level, the secret is to step back from a particular crisis in order to see the big picture, which is made up of "evening" and "morning," of difficulty and clarity. In this way I can learn to accept the ordeal and learn to deal with it, rather than fight it. If I can gain this perspective on the total or whole experience then I will have mastered the technique of laughing with one eye and crying with the other at the same time.

Since reality is made up of highs and lows then it makes sense that I learn to deal with this duality simultaneously with a smile and a sigh. Doesn't it often happen that in the midst of a good cry a friend's comforting comment will cause me to smile in the midst of my tears? I can find myself laughing and crying at the same time. This is a good model to apply when I face my next challenge.

The deeper "soul" understanding of laughing and crying simultaneously is that the crying is the laughing. Crying as a result of a painful challenge is an indication to me that the issue I am now facing is one of my key "life purpose" issues. If I then delve into my soul and try to figure out what God wants me to learn from this ordeal then I can extract a measure of personal growth and character development from the difficult situation. Thus, the crying and laughing together comprise a spiritual laughter which comes from an inner realization that I have learned an important life lesson from and through the ordeal. Working through the situation was necessary for me to move up a level in the growth of my personality. This growth leads to true inner happiness, since, as I mentioned previously, personality growth is our main purpose in life.

This is the meaning of the words we sing as part of the *Shir Hama'alot*, the psalm sung on Shabbat and Holidays before we say the *Birkat Hamazon*—the Grace After Meals: "*Hazorim b'dimah, b'rinah yiktzoru*—those who plant in tears will reap in joy" (Psalms 126:6). The traditional understanding of this verse is that if you put in effort in a project you will be rewarded in the end. This is similar to what is written in *Ethics of the Fathers*, "According to the effort is the reward" (5:26).

The Kotzker Rebbe, an 18th century chasidic leader, provides a unique insight into the verse in Psalms. He says the way to read this verse is to put the comma after the third word, *rinah*—joy, and thus read the verse as follows, "*Hazorim b'dima b'rinah, yiktzoru*—those who plant in tears and joy—will reap."

This means that life is composed of hybrid emotions and feelings. Happy and sad, trying and cathartic, painful and joyous—and these conflicting emotions can be felt by each of us simultaneously. We have to learn to be able to continue on our life's journey while carrying within us often heavy baggage of painful moments and difficult challenges.

In the *Shema Yisroel* prayer, which is a Jew's daily declaration of faith, God calls Himself Hashem and *Elokeinu*. The name "Hashem" has within it the words past, present and future—*haya*, *hoveh* and *yehieh*. This means that Hashem is All Merciful, because even though something may not be right for us in the present, it will work out in the future and, in retrospect, it will be viewed by us to have been the best thing for us.

God is *Harachaman*—the Merciful One—because He sees the Big Picture. If we are to relate to Him as Merciful, then we also have to step into the Big Picture mode and try to see things in perspective. God also calls Himself *Elokeinu*—which refers to His attribute of *din* (strict justice). Sometimes He has to treat us as a disciplining parent and we have to endure a feeling that God is relating to us sternly.

But, at the end of the first verse of the *Shema* we say "*Hashem echad*—Hashem is one.*" Both ways of His relating to us are real-ly one way. It is *all* Hashem—it is all merciful. That which we see as God's strictness is really a process of refinement that God is putting us through—for our own ultimate growth, for our own benefit. If the purpose of life is to become the most caring, sen-sitive, giving person I can be, then going through these ordeals can develop my sense of empathy for others, which will help me achieve my life's purpose. Going through life's ups and downs will soften and sensitize me to life's priorities and develop with-in me an inner tranquility—a sense of inner spiritual calm.

23

THE SECRET
OF LIFE

THE SECRET OF LIFE is to understand the model or process of how things happen in general and apply the model to your own situation. There are three phases in the process or model. Phase One is an exciting, euphoric, high moment which is a gift—a freebie—an undeserved handout which was unearned. Phase Two is the moment when the euphoria, high excitement and high feeling dissipates and the "high" turns to a mundane, difficult and trying time. Phase Three is the return of the high feeling, only now it is mine, deserved and earned rather than having been a handout or freebie. Here are a few examples.

Phase One: Your eyes meet across a crowded room. Instant attraction. Fireworks. Chemistry. You keep hearing the theme song of the Titanic playing as you walk down the street together.

Infatuation. Courtship. Romance. Falling in Love. This phase is a freebie. Did you work for it or did you deserve to "happen" to have your eyes meet? Did you work at being set up by friends or was it a chance meeting at a Shabbat table, school, college or a get-together? It's a free, undeserved handout. It's an unearned gift. Enjoy it!

Phase Two: Commitment. Then a ring. Then marriage. Then reality sets in. Why did you leave the cap off of the toothpaste? Why didn't you call to say that you would be late? Why can't you be more supportive of me when I'm "down." You don't bring me flowers anymore. This is the trying phase—when the excitement of the courtship/honeymoon period wears off in order to give the couple the chance to work through issues and make the relationship work, through their own efforts.

It is at this point when many couples in our new and improved, "throw away diaper" society, break up. When the going gets tough… I'm out of here… When the romance, the good times and the fun of the relationship are not "good" for me anymore—I walk. The secret is to work through the differences in upbringing and think of how to "make things work." Phase One was a gift/freebie in order to taste how good my relationship could possibly be. Then the magic is taken away to allow the couple to work for and earn the gift of the relationship. They work on themselves and the relationship and make it their own.

Phase Three: The couple achieve a working modus operandi in the relationship whereby they begin to understand each other and their respective needs. The couple learn to be giving to each other rather than being "takers." They learn to delete from their vocabulary such notions as, "What have you done for me lately?"

They learn to understand the way the other person thinks and thus learn to respect one another while not necessarily agreeing with each other. The relationship now begins to bond and gel. It flows. The relationship now "belongs" to the couple. They have earned the success in the relationship through hard work, each working on his or her own personality and self-control. It may take three, five or ten years. They recreate the feelings they experienced in Phase One, only now, the feelings are more grounded and based in reality rather than infatuation and fantasy.

The same three-phase model applies to a new job or project. Even though I got good grades in school, secured positive recommendations and got some good work experience, at the end of the day I've got to be in the right place at the right time, and that usually has nothing to do with my own deserving efforts. At first I am offered the job having been headhunted or chosen from among many applicants. Congratulations! Did you earn this opportunity? It is a freebie. That's Phase One. Then deadlines set in. I have to make the success happen. I have to earn the freebie. That's Phase Two. Then, when I meet the deadline and achieve success, the job or project become "mine." That's Phase Three.

The secret of life is that precisely at the moment when the excitement, euphoria and high of Phase One begins to wane, this is precisely the moment to "hang in there" and invest more energy, effort and time in making it work.

At the moment when many people give up on a relationship, when I might say, "This is not for me," that is *exactly* the moment to keep going and keep trying. Otherwise the relationship is not mine. I have to make it mine by digging deep into my spiritual center, and reflecting on how I can change myself, rather than change the situation or my partner. The challenge is sent to me not to break me but to re-create me. It is up to me to re-create myself. To walk away without a full, concerted and spirited effort is to miss the point of the challenge.

A MYSTICAL PERSPECTIVE

THE SECRET OF LIFE model can thus be summarized as follows:

Phase 1: A person receives a freebie—i.e., an undeserved gift or handout.

Phase 2: The euphoria from the undeserved freebie begins to dissipate so that the person can begin to earn the original handout through his or her own effort.

Phase 3: The person arrives at a new level of "self."

In actual fact it is God Who gives us the freebie in the first place. At first God allows us to taste how sweet romance can be by introducing us to our future mates, allowing us the wondrous experience of courtship, "falling in love," the wedding and honeymoon. Then, no sooner than we taste the sweetness of the honeymoon, God purposely brings us down to the reality of setting up a home, bills, and "how come you don't pick up after yourself."

It is God, then, who removes the euphoric honeymoon feeling so that we can start earning the rights to the original free handout. When we work through the issues, then we earn the success of the relationship through our own efforts and arrive at a new level of the relationship.

The secret of life is that as soon as we feel the euphoria of Phase 1 waning, it is precisely then that we must realize that God is challenging us to maintain our faith and to begin *earning* our freebie or undeserved handout. At the point when most people give up, that is *precisely* the moment that we should be exerting extra effort to "hang in there" during Phase 2 so that we can arrive at Phase 3, which is a new and even more rewarding level.

The source of this model can be found in the Torah, as follows:

Phase 1: The Israelites were taken out of Egypt by God's outstretched arm through the ten plagues and the splitting of the sea, even though they did not deserve to be redeemed. They had forgotten the ways of their forbears, Abraham, Isaac and Jacob and engaged in the worship of idols much the same as their Egyptian overlords. God gave them a freebie or undeserved handout by redeeming them anyway. He did this because of His original promise to Abraham that He would one day redeem Abraham's descendants and bring them to the Promised Land.

Phase 2: After experiencing the splitting of the sea and the euphoria of freedom from their oppressors, the Israelites had to face the prospect of living in the harsh Sinai desert. Although the clouds of glory protected them from the elements to a great extent, nevertheless, they had to face their share of difficulties. They had to come to terms with their freedom by maintaining their faith in God *despite* their ordeals, thereby earning their previously undeserved freedom.

Phase 3: After wrestling with their faith in God in the desert the Israelites arrived at Mount Sinai to receive the Ten Commandments from God. They earned their right to receive this Blueprint of Life after their struggle through the desert which earned them their spiritual redemption, although the exodus from Egypt was their physical redemption. The desert experience allowed them to earn their spiritual redemption. Receiving the Ten Commandments was their spiritual reward.

Many people throughout history have been inspired by the Israelites' Exodus from slavery in Egypt. Thomas Jefferson wanted to use the Exodus scene as the motif of the founding of the United States of America. The Civil Rights movement identified their quest for equal rights as a reenactment of the Israelites' quest for freedom.

We are in fact the most free society in history. The question we must ask ourselves, however, is, what are we doing with our freedom? Are we making use of our time in this world constructively or are we just passing the time? When God challenges us with issues and crises, He is "speaking to us" and urging us to rethink our priorities so that we will use our lives for a meaningful purpose. When God presents us with a difficulty, He is challenging us to "work for our supper" and to redouble our efforts to make our lives count. God does not want us to enjoy *nehama d'kisufa* (bread of shame), which means reward without effort. That, in fact, is why God created this world as a world of striving and travail—so that we can earn our reward in the World to Come.

The *Midrash* tells us that Moses had a "dialogue" with the Red Sea as the Israelites approached it during the time they were being chased by the Egyptians. Moses told the sea to split. The sea responded that it would not as it was fulfilling God's will by flowing in its natural state just as God had commanded when He created the sea on the second day of creation. When, however, the sea saw the coffin of Joseph *Hatzaddik*—Joseph the Righteous—approaching, the Book of Psalms states, *"hayam raah vayanos*—The sea saw and it fled"* (Psalms 114:3).

Joseph's greatness, and the reason he is called Joseph

Hatzaddik, was that he went against his natural inclination and resisted the seductive advances of Potiphar's wife. The Torah states: "But he left his garment in her hand, and he fled..." (Genesis 39:12). The sea saw that Joseph rose above his "nature"—so it too could go against its "nature" and stop flowing naturally—to allow the Israelites to cross through the sea. Since Joseph "fled," the sea too "fled"—and split.

As I've mentioned, our purpose in life is to overcome and to grow in character and personal refinement. We cannot say: "Well, that's the way God made me. I'm short tempered, lazy, unmotivated, it's just the way I am." We were created in order to develop our natural tendencies, not to become entrenched in them. Our job is to take charge of our personalities and to change our natural way of doing things in order to achieve our potential.

24

THE NON-COMMITMENT SYNDROME

A SPIRITUAL PERSPECTIVE

IT USED TO BE THAT young men and women would go to social clubs at the local Y or community center and develop a social network from which they would choose a spouse. Usually they were in their early or mid-twenties. Commitment wasn't a problem. It was something everyone did. Settle down, have a few kids, struggle with a mortgage, get aggravated by your mother-in-law. Then you know that you've joined the establishment.

Today there's a singles scene that has grown, which does not serve as a network for marriage. Rather, it perpetuates itself for the twenty- and thirty-somethings, and becomes a stage of life that is fast, fun and commitment free. Our singles learn that there is always going to be someone better looking, with a nicer car and a better job at the next party, so why settle? I want the best. I deserve it.

At some point in this singles scene, most people will decide to settle down and it is at this point they may have a problem. I know of one man in his mid-thirties who decided he ought to settle down because he was getting tired of the singles scene, he saw some friends with little kids, and besides, he'd been there, done that, bought the T shirt….more of the same would get boring. So he decided to stick with one woman for two years, but he isn't able to make the ultimate commitment. So he sees me or a psychologist, an advisor or a close friend. "I just can't commit. I don't want to be locked in." Once you've been in a non-commitment mode, it is hard to make that giant leap of faith into a single, loyal, committed relationship. What you have to look at, I said to him, is not what you are giving up but what you will be *gaining*.

Remember when you wrote that love letter to your sweetheart so many thousands of years ago? You wrote: "I would swim the deepest sea, I would climb the highest mountain…."

What you meant was that you were willing—in the midst of that time of love and inspiration—to make a commitment to do anything, go anywhere, support and "be there" for your sweetheart. It meant you were willing to "hang in there" for the long term and work through life together. You were willing to sacrifice and give of yourself to be with that person. It meant much more than a fleeting romance or infatuation. It was meant to last and to grow.

The long-term (what a tough word for a non-committer) benefits of a loyal, committed relationship are depth of the relationship and living through the seasons of challenge together. Going through the ups and downs of life together over a period of time makes me focus not solely on myself and my own needs but on something "bigger" than myself, namely, the relationship.

If I shift my focus from what the good life can give me to what I can do to develop someone else, then the relationship becomes stronger and deeper. I become less self-centered and more "other" oriented. This will lead to the growth of my character as a more giving and nurturing individual. If the purpose of life is my personal happiness, then I can see why it would be almost impossible to give up single life. If, however, I re-evaluate my perceptions of the purpose of life as "how meaningful my life can be" then it would be much easier to break the non-commitment syndrome.

What about maintaining commitment during a longer term relationship? What about the "seven year itch"? Isn't it natural to have the excitement of a relationship wane? Is it true that there is an adultery gene?

These are merely man-made excuses or challenges to the depth of the relationship. When sex is seen as my right then it can be misused. If I see sex as a means to further develop the love in a relationship and to give pleasure rather than merely to receive pleasure, then sex would not be a major factor in marital breakdown, as it is today according to statistics. Sex becomes a tool to make the marriage "other" centered, rather than "self" centered.

One of the ways to convert sex into a builder of the relationship is to follow Masters and Johnson's suggestion of abstaining from sex for a week after the end of menstruation. This would give a couple the opportunity to see themselves as "persons" again rather than only as sexual beings. It would give them an opportunity to work out certain issues which were glossed over and not dealt with and it will also create a sexual tension within the marriage which will allow the couple to see each other as lovers and restore the courtship element again. It would give the sexual dimension of the marriage a rhythm and an actual renewal and rejuvenation every two weeks. Imagine the passion when intimate relations are resumed after twelve days of abstinence, (presuming the kids are asleep—little chance of that!). It would restore the honeymoon atmosphere to the relationship. A monthly honeymoon sure beats a "second honeymoon" after thirty years of marriage.

A MYSTICAL PERSPECTIVE

THE RELATIONSHIP THAT GOD has created with the Jewish people is known as a bris—a covenant. This is more than a contract in which the obligations are interdependent. If one party fails to fulfill his or her obligations the other party is "off the hook" and the contract is over. Not so with a covenant. God is committed to His being our God, even if we fail to keep our part of the bargain. However, the ideal is to strive to keep the covenant, even if supper is burnt or if my spouse gets laid off.

In his last challenge to the Jewish people, Moses said,

"It is not in the heavens for you to say, 'Who can ascend to the Heavens for us and take it for us, and let us hear it, so that we can perform it?' Nor is it across the sea for you to say, 'Who can cross to the other side of the sea for us and take it for us and let us hear it so that we can perform it?' Rather, the matter is very near to you, in your mouth and in your heart, to perform it." (Deuteronomy 30:12-14)

We do not even have to "swim the deepest sea," or "climb

the highest mountain" to reach God. The matter is very near to us. It is within our power to make the commitment to engage God in an ongoing daily relationship by following the Torah.

When we plow our fields, we can't plow with an ox and a donkey together since that would be cruel to both animals. When we harvest our fields, we must leave the corners of the field for the poor. When we knead our dough, we must give a portion to the *kohein* (priest). When we shear the sheep and make clothes, Jewish males are obligated to wear *tzitzis* (fringes) on the corners to help them remember that our gift of clothing comes with "strings attached" and that our clothing comes from God. When we build a house, we must make a parapet on the roof and place a *mezuzah* on the door. In every aspect of our lives we can engage God and sanctify every moment and every thing. It is all encompassing and all pervasive. This requires commitment.

Another word for commitment is loyalty. The more we act with loyalty, the more we will be bonded in the relationship. The more we give in the relationship, the more we will love the other person. Hold it! Isn't that the wrong way round? Aren't you supposed to love someone and then develop the desire to bond and to give to them? No.

When Isaac married Rebecca, the Torah states, "And he married her and then he loved her" (Genesis 24:67). Isn't this a bit out of date? Doesn't love come first, then marriage? The Torah is teaching us an important lesson here. If we share the same world-view with our spouse and we commit ourselves to work together to fulfill that jointly held world view, then we will come to love our spouse as a result of working with him or her to fulfill that goal.

Rebecca and Isaac shared the same world view—they both wanted to build a new way of life committed to serving God and creating a family which would follow in the footsteps of Abraham and Sarah. The commitment itself produced love between them for each other. First they were married and then love followed as a result of their working on the goals of their marriage.

Rebecca and Isaac didn't have to fall in love first, and then marry. They were committed to the essence of loving Jewishly—which means giving and sacrificing for each other. They followed the Torah ideal that we love the people to whom we give, rather than give to the people we love. The more we give to our spouse, the more we will come to love him or her. Even though this goes against conventional wisdom, it *does* work. Let me explain.

When we say, "I love fish," what are we really saying? If we really loved fish we would have various aquariums in our homes and breed, nurture and speak to our fish, like we speak to our plants. We would not catch, skin, gut, fry and eat the fish with tartar sauce—this fish that we profess to "love."

So, when we say we love fish, we are really saying that we love how the fish satiates us and makes us feel. And it makes us feel good—so we love it.

"I love fish" means I love what the fish does for *me*. Apply this reasoning to the word "love" that we use in our contemporary relationships. When we say "I love you," what we are really saying is, "I love the way you make me feel. I love the way you care for me, your friendship and your intimacy. As long as you continue to make me feel good I will continue to do for you." This, however, does not make for a lasting relationship. This attitude of "love" we use so much today has led to a fifty percent divorce rate. Obviously, there is something wrong with our attitude toward "love."

A more effective attitude toward love is the Torah model. The more we give to and are committed and loyal to our spouses, the more we will come to love him or her. The more we sustain a loyalty to our spouse, despite the ups and downs of the relationship, the stronger the bond will grow. Commitment is a deeper level of relationship than "chemistry" or infatuation. The feeling of "being in love" is more about *me* than about my partner. The true and deeper meaning of love is how we make the other person feel rather than how they make us feel. The essence of love is not "and what have you done for me lately?" but "what have I done for you, lately?"

Love is about how much we have been there for our spouse. The closeness we feel with our spouse is up to us. We must take responsibility for the relationship by placing ourselves in the "giving" rather than the "receiving" mode.

The Hebrew word for love is *ahava*, which means "to give." The essence of loving Jewishly is *giving*. Isaac and Rebecca were committed to giving to each other within their marriage, so they married themselves to the concept of giving to each other and then they loved each other.

Within marriage, the relationship is strengthened by making intimacy into a bonding mechanism—a means to an end. Sex is tool to give to my spouse, not to receive. The Torah system for intimacy within marriage, known as *Taharat Hamishpacha*—Family Purity—requires a period of separation between spouses so that they are not intimate with each other during the menstrual cycle, plus a further seven days. During this time, the couple relate to each other emotionally and yearn for each other physically which develops the bond between them.

In this way the "needs" and "desires" of the parties are sublimated to the overall needs of the unit or the relationship. By making a marriage commitment, the couple is adding a third Godly element to the relationship. By adding God to the equation it is no longer what I think or what you think—but what is best for the relationship. The spiritual dimension comes from beyond the relationship and adds a transcendent spark of Godliness and purity to the everyday relationship.

25

LIVING LIFE TO
THE FULLEST

A SPIRITUAL PERSPECTIVE

WHEN I WAS TWELVE AND growing up in Montreal, Canada, I remember getting into my parent's car on a Sunday morning as my family was preparing for a day trip to the beach in Massena, New York. I was watching my younger sister and brother walk toward the car with their sand pails and shovels and I remember asking myself, "I wonder when life is going to start?" At the same moment, I answered my own question. "This is life. Going to the beach with my family on a Sunday…it doesn't get any more real…it doesn't get any better."

The moment I am experiencing right now is the most important moment of my life. I can appreciate, learn from and be in awe of this moment. That will cause the moment to last. If I do this for each moment or event then I will be "living life to the fullest."

A MYSTICAL PERSPECTIVE

LIFE SEEMS TO FLY BY. I try to live in the moment but it is already behind me. It seems that John Lennon got it right when he wrote, "Life is what happens to me when I'm planning something else."

How can I "seize the moment" then? Is it a fiction, just beyond my grasp?

I can capture the moment by allowing God into the moment, since God is the Creator of Time, as the Torah states, "In the beginning God created..." (Genesis 1:1).

He is the One Who began the beginning. He created and began time. As the Creator of time, He is thus beyond Time, while human beings operate within the framework of time. I, however, can capture a particular moment in time by making God part of the experience, and thus spiritualize and eternalize the moment.

When Jacob went to Egypt to meet his son Joseph, who he had not seen for twenty-two years, the Torah says that they embraced and that "Joseph cried on his father's shoulder." (Genesis 46:29). It does not say what Jacob was doing. Rashi says that Jacob was reciting a prayer at that moment. The prayer was the declaration of faith, the *Shema Yisroel*: "Hear O Israel, the Lord our God, the Lord is One" (Deuteronomy 6:4).

The moment was so emotionally charged that Jacob wanted to make the moment last forever. He wanted to infuse this personal, human moment with Godly spirituality. He ensured that the moment would be concretized by dedicating that moment to God by saying the *Shema*—which is the Jew yearning to touch eternity. The Torah's message is that we, too, can make moments last by spiritualizing them. A small prayer at a moment of high emotion will add this spiritual element.

The Torah teaches us how we can actualize our potential by emulating our spiritual ancestors. The Torah states, "And the years of Sarah's life were one hundred years and twenty years and seven years" (Genesis 23:1).

The Biblical commentator Rashi asks, why did the Torah choose to calculate the years of Sarah's life as one hundred, twenty and seven, rather than as one hundred and twenty-seven? He explains that Sarah was able to live every moment of each phase of her life to the fullest. She lived her senior years—her "one hundred" years to the fullest. *Ziknah*—the Hebrew word for old age is an acronym for—*zeh she'kanah chochmah*—one who has acquired wisdom. She lived her youth, represented by her "twenties" with a mature youthfulness—channeling her energies into well conceived, meaningful and worthwhile projects by bringing *chesed* (loving-kindness) to the world, teaching the world about Godliness and raising her son, Isaac, to be the continuity of belief in the Creator. Her "seven" years represents a child's innocence which she maintained throughout her life. Furthermore, the verse connects each of the sections of her life with a "*vav*"—the word "and," which means that she linked the values of innocence throughout her youthfulness and senior years. She linked her maturity to her older years by dedicating her entire life to worthwhile endeavors.

The *Midrash* takes this idea one step deeper. The *Midrash* states, "Rabbi Akiva said, 'Why did Queen Esther merit becoming queen over one-hundred and twenty-seven provinces? Let Esther come, the granddaughter of Sarah, who lived one hundred, and twenty and seven years, and let her rule over one hundred and twenty seven provinces'" (Genesis Rabbah 58:3). The *Midrash* is teaching us here that the secret to becoming successful at the art of living, and to rule over the provinces of wealth and personal success, is to use *every* moment, *every* year of your life wisely and fully. Of all the grandchildren of Sarah—and all the prophetesses, who are also "grandchildren" of Sarah, the *Midrash* singled out Esther to show us that to become king or queen, which means to "rule" over one's life in terms of personal success, is dependent on using our time—our precious time, wisely.

26

LIVING LIFE IN
THE PRESENT

A SPIRITUAL PERSPECTIVE

MOVIES AND TELEVISION programs have a built in mechanism to help you "wake up and pay attention" and to let you know when the good part is coming. It is the background music. When there is suspense and adventure, we hear exciting, tense, music. When there is a tragic moment, we hear melancholy music. In a love story, we hear a flowing, romantic symphony. Thus, the television producer helps us react to a scene on the screen with the help of the music which sets the tone of our mood.

In real life, however, there is no background music to help us wake up when the important parts of our life are about to happen. There is no background music to alert us as to how or when to "get ready" for the moment when you are called upon to dramatically act or react. So, without the help of a sound mixer for our lives, how do we know when the important moments of our life are taking place?

I have to admit that at least once during the past year I prayed to win the lottery. In my imaginary world of "well, someone has to win" I fantasized as to what I would do with the money. I suppose it's worth the dollar to step into dream mode for a moment. It is good to dream. It allows me to transport myself beyond my present turmoil. It gives me a sense of hope that I won't necessarily be stuck in my current mess forever. However, I cannot live in the fantasy future. I must learn to live now in my present reality.

Memories about the "good old days" and warm thoughts of good times past are important. I can indulge in thinking about them because those events are now part of my psyche. They have shaped me and made me into what I am today. By drawing on the feelings that these memories evoke I can gain strength to weather my current challenges. "I've been through worse," I could tell myself.

Fond memories of playing soccer-baseball* in our backyard in Montreal with my brother and sister give me the encouragement that nostalgia creates. I remember that the broken steps on the hill were first base, the Silver Maple tree was second and the Norway Maple was third. I remember all the neighborhood kids playing in our backyard after supper on those long summer evenings. These memories are not only pleasant, they spur me on to recreate those feelings by playing soccer-baseball with my own kids in our backyard in Baltimore.

I remember, for instance, planting a vegetable garden with

---

*For those who may not have heard of it—trust me, this *is* a sport.

my Dad in our backyard when I was ten. He dug up a patch of earth near the fence and turned over the soil. He added some black topsoil and made rows. Then he showed me how to make a furrow at the top of the row of black earth and had me plant radish seeds, one in each hole at five-inch intervals. I couldn't imagine how these tiny seeds would ever produce healthy radishes so, when he wasn't looking I disobeyed his instructions and put five seeds in each hole and we ended up with serious radish overcrowding. If only I knew then what I know now I would have listened to my father's voice of experience.

That's it! The purpose of memories is to use my experience in order to live better now! Last summer I dug up a patch of earth by the fence in our backyard. I added some black topsoil and made rows and taught my kids how to make a furrow at top of the row. I instructed my ten-year-old son to put one radish seed into each hole and I pretended not to notice as he sprinkled five seeds into each hole. I didn't say a word. Wasn't it only yesterday that my Dad was teaching me how to plant a vegetable garden? That night I phoned my Dad long distance and told him the story. We both had a good cry.

Thus the purpose of the past is to allow me to recreate and to improve on my present. It is not to "live" in the past. Although I try to capture the present moment (the Latin expression is *carpe diem*—seize the day), I can't. The moment ahead of me is still in the future. As soon as it comes into view and I try to "grab it" it is already behind me, already in the past. My challenges, however, force me to face the present and to live now. I can draw upon past victories and memories to help me deal with the present. I can dream about the future to propel me beyond my current and present pain. The focus, however, must be on the present reality.

I must learn to appreciate the nuances of the "here and now" instead of the "there and then." I can do this by giving my full attention to the person I am speaking to. I can gently focus on their eyes, saying, in effect, "I'm here for you." So the most important moment in my life is right now. The circumstance I am in right now *is* the background music that urges me to take note and appreciate life as it is happening.

A MYSTICAL PERSPECTIVE

WHEN ASKED BY A roving reporter: "So, what's the most important thing in your life?" the conscience ridden among us will answer: "My family…my sweet little children…my spouse…" "Oh really?" the reporter will say, "is that why you consistently stay late hours at the office, work weekends, spend time out with friends and when your kids ask you to pitch around a baseball you say: 'I'm busy…I'm exhausted…I'm unwinding, reading the newspaper….maybe later.'" And later keeps on getting later, every year.

I was traveling home on the Toronto subway during my law days and met a fellow lawyer who was on the same train. We engaged in small talk and then I noticed that he was carrying two briefcases. "I'm bringing work home…this briefcase is for Susie and this one is for Janie," he said, holding up the briefcases one by one. "Oh really?" I said to myself. "And when you work so hard to make all this money for Susie and Janie did you ever stop and think that they'd probably forgo that extra trinket, holiday, or doll for a few extra minutes with their dad?" "Not now honey…can't you see I'm busy making money for you so that you can have a better life?!" I suppose in the end it all depends on your definition of "a better life."

When are we ever going to learn that life is *not* a matter of history—what happened twenty years ago—or the distant future… "when I fulfill my dream I'm gonna,"—rather it's happening right now—in the here and now. The only way to shock ourselves back into the present is to get in touch with God, Who Lives in the present, past and future at the same time.

The *Shema Yisroel* prayer tells us, "*V'hayu hadevarim ha'eylah asher Anochi metzavchah hayom al levavecha*—These words which I command you today shall be on your heart" (Deuteronomy 6:6).

Rashi comments, "These words should not be like a king's old edict, rather, *k'chadash*—new—as if they were commanded today." Our observance of Judaism—our relationship with God—should have a feeling of freshness, vitality and newness, as if we ourselves heard God command us to keep the Torah at Mount Sinai. Our relationship with God must be alive, in the present tense, as all of our relationships should be.

In the *Yehi Chvod* psalm which is said in the morning prayers, before we say the *Ashrei*, we declare, "*Hashem melech, Hashem malach, Hashem yimloch…Hashem melech olam vaed*—God reigns, God has reigned, God shall reign…God reigns forever." If the verse, which is a compilation of different verses from Psalms and the Prophets, already mentioned God reigning in the past, present and future, then why begin the next praise of "God reigns"—in the present tense?

The answer must be that there is a difference between theory and practice. Of course, God is beyond time. That is my awe of God's transcendence. But how am I to relate to Him in practice?

As *Hashem melech*—as the God Who lives in the here and

now. Which means I have to get my act together *now*—and live wholly in the present. This means that whatever situation I am in, the present is the most important situation or moment of my life. My discussion with my wife, my doing homework with my kids, talking to their school teacher or an employee, I have to be "all there" for that person, otherwise I am not giving all I can to the person, which means I am not getting all I can from the encounter because I am not living in the here and now.

The *Midrash* illustrates this point with searing depth as follows: If Reuben had known that the Torah would record how he dealt with his brothers' attempts to "deal" with Joseph, then he would have placed Joseph on his shoulders and brought him to his father. Had Aaron known that the Torah would describe his reunion with his brother Moses on his return to Egypt, to begin leading the Jewish people out of Egypt, he would have greeted him with cymbals, tambourines, song and dance. Had Boaz known that the *Megillah* would record how he treated Ruth, then he would have given her wagonloads of grain and produce (Midrash Ruth Rabbah 5:6).

When we do something, in the midst of our daily situations, we think that our behavior is mundane, ordinary and unnoticed. In actual fact everything we say and do is recorded by God's big VCR in the sky. The *Midrash* concludes that our actions are recorded by Elijah the prophet and the *Mashiach*—the Messiah—and that God Himself signs the record.

We must realize that *life is happening now*. We are living and writing our own history—a living history. On Rosh Hashanah and Yom Kippur in the powerful *Unesaneh Tokef* prayer where we ask, "who will live and who will die....", as it says in the Talmud: "*V'yad kol adam chosam bo*—and the hand of each person signs the decree" (Taanith 11a). We sign the decree. We create our own priorities and our own agenda for life. God has empowered us to write our own destiny and then He personally guides and direct us in response to our choices.

If we could live on this level—that our lives, our histories— are being written and shaped by our words and actions in the present moment, then each moment will take on new meaning and each act we perform will take on new significance for us.

There is a beautiful story told of a rebbe of a fifth grade class who played a game with his students. The student would hide something in his hand, and the rebbe, knowing the students very well, would guess what the student had in his hand. A rock, a leaf, a sharpener. One day, Yossi told his friends he was going to stump the rebbe. He would choose a butterfly. The rebbe, knowing Yossi's love for butterflies, would, of course, guess that it was a butterfly. "But then," said Yossi, "I will ask the rebbe— but rebbe, is the butterfly dead or alive? If he says it is alive I will squish it and he will be wrong. If he says it is dead, I'll open my hand and release it. Either way, the rebbe will be wrong."

All the boys crowded around the rebbe as Yossi approached for the big moment. "Rebbe, what do I have in my hand?" asked Yossi. "You have a butterfly, of course," answered the rebbe. "But, rebbe, is it dead or alive?" asked Yossi with anticipation. The rebbe looked at Yossi, and answered with a smile: "My dear Yossi…it's what you make of it."

Life is in your hands. It is what you make of it.

27

LIVE A LITTLE

COME ON, LIGHTEN UP and live a little. You only live once, you know. Besides the trying moments, and to be sure, there are many, there are also light and airy moments—if we only learn to let our hair down—and live a little.

But I thought the purpose of life is to grow and become the best person I can be, so how does that jive with "light and airy?" First, even in the midst of a challenge I must be able to step back and smile at myself, while I am going through this trying moment. "Here we go again," you could say to yourself, "what now?" Only say it with a wry smile, the kind of feeling you have when you arrive at the top of the water log ride at the theme park, the one your kids convinced you to go on, but you didn't really want to. You get to the top of the steep incline, just before the log begins hurtling down the water ramp at sixty miles an hour, and your mouth goes into your stomach and at that moment you smile to yourself and say: "Here we go…who got me into this mess?" But you say it with a smile, sort of laughing at yourself in the predicament. It's like the "grin and bear it" expression on the face of the man on the cover of this book. Now, that's the attitude you should have going into the next "challenge"—a bit of tongue in cheek—hang on for the ride because this is what is being presented to you right now.

Secondly, there are the light moments. Picnics with the family, sitting in the backyard on a summer afternoon watching your kids play in the kiddie pool, walking along the boardwalk at some holiday spot with your spouse, hoping that the kids who are farmed out to four different families are okay—but take it easy—you're on vacation. So live a little—you're entitled!

These moments are important because they help put life into perspective. It's not all challenge, crisis and ordeal. You are allowed to enjoy yourself in life. You are, in fact, obligated to! Enjoying life means you appreciate being alive and you are happy to be part of the world. It is a happy and carefree feeling. We need such moments to stay sane.

In August 1999 there was a total eclipse of the sun which could be seen along a pathway in Europe including England, where we then lived. A woman I knew who witnessed the eclipse, said that watching the moment of totality with the earth plunged into darkness for two minutes in the middle of the day made her aware that the cosmos did actually affect her personally. It made her feel privileged to be part of this amazing universe.

While I was moved by her sentiments I asked her why it took the once-in-a-lifetime experience of watching an eclipse for her to be in awe of the universe and become aware of her part in it? Is the daily sunrise, the thunderstorm, ocean waves and watching the tulips close up at night any less miraculous than the spectacle of the eclipse? Aren't everyday miracles also miracles? Sure, but we have become desensitized to them because they happen constantly.

There's the secret! Don't allow yourself to become desensitized to the everyday joys of life. You don't have to wait for a Bar Mitzvah, wedding or graduation to be "happy." You can learn to be happy watching your kids run down the street, interacting with the kids while you're sprawled out on the floor playing Monopoly, or going for a walk with your spouse around the block at night when the kids are asleep on a hot summer's night. Happiness is an everyday thing. Being aware of these small, everyday happinesses, will make everyday life more enjoyable. So, lighten up and get a life!

A MYSTICAL PERSPECTIVE

WE ARE UNDER THE impression that God's first commandment to us was a negative precept, "Do not eat from the tree of knowledge of good and evil." *Wrong.*

God's first commandment was: *"Mikol etz Hagan achol tochel—From every tree of the Garden you shall surely eat"* (Genesis 2:16). The Torah commentary, the *Meshech Chochmah**, comments on this verse that the double language of *"achol tochel—you shall surely eat"* does not mean that you *may* eat. It

---

*Rabbi Meir Simcha of Dvinsk (1843-1926).

means that you *must* eat. It is a mitzvah to eat. This means it is a mitzvah to partake and enjoy of the pleasures of this world. Basically God is saying to us: Live a little!

The Jerusalem Talmud states that when we arrive in the next world we will have to give an accounting for all those pleasures that God gave us but that we did not take advantage of and enjoy (Kiddushin 48b).

God wants us to enjoy life's pleasures not for their own sake but to attribute them to their source—to God Himself. Enjoy food, but acknowledge the Source by making a *bracha*—a blessing. Enjoy intimacy with your spouse—but follow the laws and framework of *taharas hamishpacha*—family purity. Enjoy the pleasures—but use them for a higher purpose—to enhance and develop your relationship with God, *the Source* of all pleasure.

The Torah is in love with the world. It is not in opposition to the world. We have a tendency to focus on the restrictive aspects of the Torah—the "don'ts" instead of the joyful aspects and the "do's."

The don'ts are there to liberate us from being enslaved to our animalistic lusts and passions. Once we are liberated from these by gaining mastery over our impulses and auto pilot instincts, then we can actualize our potential by bringing out the best in ourselves through the positive commandments.

The word *yirah* is often translated as fear of God. The *Mesilas Yesharim—The Path of the Just,* written by Rabbi Moshe Chaim Luzatto in the 18th century, teaches us that "fear of punishment" is only the first level of *yirah*. The second, and higher level is *yiras haromemus*—awe of grandeur, majesty and ultimate power of God. A Jewish way of life puts us into a constant state of amazement and awe of God's world and makes us constantly aware that we have a significant part to play on His stage.

When the brilliant German Jewish thinker Rabbi Samson Raphael Hirsch was in his nineties he took a trip to the Swiss Alps. His students were very concerned that a man of his advanced age and frailty would take such a dangerous trip—and to go sightseeing in his nineties?! Rabbi Hirsch answered his students: "After 120 years God will ask me: 'Samson, did you hear of my great Alps?' I will say: 'Of course!' and God will then say: 'Then why didn't you go see them so that you could say *mah rabu maasecha Hashem*—how wondrous are your works, O God?" (Psalms 104:24).

28

BRIDGING THE
GENERATION GAP

A SPIRITUAL PERSPECTIVE

IN 1997, JOHN MAJOR, then the Prime Minister of Britain, traveled to India on a State visit. While there, he went to the mountain areas to visit an ancient tribe which inhabits the mountain range between India and Tibet. He attended a very moving "coming of age" ceremony of a particular tribe whereby a group of thirteen-year-old boys were being welcomed as "Men" into the tribe. It was their initiation or confirmation ritual.

The Prime Minister watched as the father of each boy walked up to his son and presented him with a symbol of manhood and tribal identity—a Kalashnikov rifle. This ceremony speaks volumes about the values of the society, highlighting their most important value—self-preservation amidst the warring mountain tribes and communal pride in taking part in the defense of the values of the tribe.

During Passover of 1999, I too experienced a coming of age ceremony—American style. My family and I were spending Passover with my in laws in Memphis, Tennessee. It was extra special to us because my parents flew down to Memphis from Montreal to spend the holidays with us. It was literally the first time that my kids were able to spend time with both sets of their grandparents at the same time, as we then lived in England. (So, let's not take those routine family visits for granted!)

During the middle of the holiday I took my son, who was then nine, and my dad, to a sporting goods store so that my dad could advise me on the purchase of my son's first baseball glove (in England, you see, we played only soccer and cricket).

There we were in the middle of the baseball section trying on baseball mitts and throwing some baseballs to each other in the aisle to make sure the glove was a good fit and the ball would go easily into the "pocket" of the glove.

"This is the one," said my dad finally, "and I'm paying," he added, with a beaming glow of pride. It's no small thing, you know, to get your first baseball glove. I was happy to let my dad pay because I felt like I was experiencing the continuity of an American tradition. My grandfather had bought me my first glove—and now my dad was doing the same for my son.

It meant a lot to me—that moment in the store. While trying on gloves in the store I had flashbacks of my dad and I pitching around a baseball in our Montreal backyard and my dad throwing me practice fly balls and pointers on how to backpedal when the ball was behind me. "Come on in for dinner," my mom would say. "Just two more throws, Mom," I would beg.

It was one of those warm father and son moments that I will

always remember and treasure—because it represents the connection from one generation to the next through a language we both understand—the language of baseball. My father taught me how to play as my father's father had taught him. My dad used to take me to Little League baseball games and cheer me from the stands. I was a pretty decent little pitcher. And now my dad was literally handing this "tradition" down to my son. In a small way, it was a moment and a gesture which bridged the generation gap—a special moment of connection. Now I wish bedtime was that special. Dad, maybe you could fly over and show us how Grandpa put you guys to bed. Some things never change.

I guess that is what life is all about: experiencing a little tradition and passing it on to your kids.

That was a moment of spirituality. It captured a taste of immortality. If my son passes on the tradition to his son then I could live forever...so to speak. For my dad, that moment in the store represented continuity. He witnessed and was apart of the transmission of the values that baseball represents—sportsmanship, teamwork, camaraderie—and good clean fun. For me, it meant the reliving of some warm childhood memories and instilled in me the hope that I might be able to do the same for my grandson one day. For my son, it didn't mean that much...another sport to be added to the list of badminton, soccer and cricket. But I bet it will be filed in his long-term memory which he will recall with fondness when I accompany him and his son to the baseball store in thirty years time. Only then will his own visit to buy his first glove take on real meaning for him.

What are the values that I am instilling in my kids? What things and pursuits do I hold dear that I would like to see continued into the next generation? Is it an appreciation for the finer things in life—good wine, a good restaurant, my love of baseball? Maybe it's expertise at chess or the right way to wash your car? What are the things that I can't touch or see but are the most valuable things, concepts and morals that I can transmit to my children? If I can put a finger on them wouldn't that be nothing less than figuring out what life is all about.

A MYSTICAL PERSPECTIVE

AT THE PASSOVER SEDER the number "four" is the most prevalent. Four Questions, Four Sons, Four cups of wine. Why the number four? Rabbi Nota Schiller* provided an answer: The number four refers to the Four Matriarchs—Sarah, Rebecca, Rachel and Leah. Passover represents the birth of the Jewish people and that is why motherhood—represented by the four Matriarchs—is the operative theme.

Even Jews who are estranged from Jewish life and practice have a craving to be at a Seder. Passover tugs at their spiritual umbilical chord—they feel their soul stirring—it is awakened and they want to feel the spiritual connection to their people. For it is at the Seder that we convey the love for our heritage to the next generation. We express our love not only verbally, but experientially. We show our children and feel with them the bitterness of the *maror*, and the salty tears of slavery and we taste the wine of freedom and the green vegetables of springtime and rejuvenation. We bridge the generation gap by experiencing Judaism with our children.

---

* *Rosh Yeshiva* (dean of the yeshiva) at Yeshivat Ohr Somayach in Jerusalem.

During the *Magid*, the narrative section of the *Haggadah*, we respond to the children's questions of the well-known section of *mah nishtanah*, by saying: "It is a mitzvah for us to tell about the miracles that happened when the Jews left Egypt. The more someone tells about it, the more he deserves to be praised."

Rabbi Shalom Noach Brozofsky, author of *Nesivos Shalom*, asks: Why do we expound upon the miracles of going out of Egypt? Why is it more praiseworthy to add more and more and to elaborate upon the wonders that God did for us unlike other *mitzvot*? It is not considered more praiseworthy if we shake the *lulav* all night. Nor is it considered more praiseworthy if we blow the *shofar* all morning!

The *Nesivos Shalom* answers: The Passover Seder is the *Rosh Hashanah*—the Jewish New Year for faith. The more we describe God's personal hand in redeeming us from Egypt the more we instill faith in the hearts of our children. That is why even if the children know more than the parents, it is a mitzvah for the parents to tell the story of the Exodus to their children, because the transmission of faith from parents to children on this night implants the love of God directly into the hearts of the children. This is the way we bridge the generation gap. We don't just *tell* the story to our children. We *live* the story and we lodge the faith within their souls.

29

CAN'T COMPLAIN

"HOW ARE YOU?"

"Can't complain."

"You mean you would like to complain, but, what can you do, life is going okay right now, so you can't complain?"

"*No*, I mean things are fine."

"Oh, that's great! Why didn't you say so?"

Sometimes the "can't complain" attitude reveals a negative mindset and world view. The world is my adversary and things usually go against me, but right now there is a ceasefire.

This attitude puts me into an anxious and uneasy relationship with my world. This attitude will not let me operate to my optimum capacity. I will always be in "fighting" mode as the events of my life seem to be attacking me. I get out of bed in the morning by peaking out from under the covers to see if the shooting has stopped so I can make a run for it.

A more effective and "user friendly" world view would be to say, "I'm fine, thank you. I am going with the flow. I look at life as an adventure. I get out of bed in the morning with a positive attitude looking forward to the challenges of the day. I want to learn from the day's events and I want to grow today in both character and personal wisdom."

This attitude would put me in a more productive mindset. I can achieve a feeling of inner harmony by working *with* the events of the day instead of *against* them.

A MYSTICAL PERSPECTIVE

IF THE PURPOSE OF LIFE is "to be happy" and I experience any form of discomfort, difficulty or upset then I would be correct in saying that I was not achieving my purpose in life. I would then be justified if I reacted with frustration and upset. If, however, the purpose of life is *not* "to be happy" but to become the best person I can be, then any problem, discomfort or challenge is not a contradiction to my achieving my life's purpose. Rather, it is sent to me by God to teach me something about my personality and how I can improve my character.

When I think in these terms then I begin to have a "personal relationship with God," or in short, I gain a "personal God." In this way, the complaints of my life can be transformed into opportunities for positive personal growth.

When I practiced law in Toronto, before becoming a rabbi, one of the most exciting challenges of my career was to transform a bad situation into one that could work for me. One application of this idea is when my legal case contained a flaw or weakness. I was taught to reveal the weakness, as part of my own case, rather than letting the other lawyer "drop the bomb" and destroy my case. In this way I can put the problem before the court, show my honesty in admitting I have a weakness and then explaining, justifying or putting this negative aspect into context.

This is called turning a liability into an asset. This lesson can be applied to life. We can take the difficulties of our lives and "put them on the table" and deal with them. If we address them and grow through the experience then we will be taking a liability and make it work for ourselves.

While many people may accept that there is a God who created the Universe, their next sentiment would likely be: So what does God have to do with me, personally? God is surely too busy dealing with global warming, ethnic cleansing and the threat of nuclear war to have time for me. But He does.

If we would take the concept of God's omnipotence to its logical conclusion, we would realize that God *does* have time for everyone. This is what is meant by Divine Providence. God is not only the Creator but He is also the Guide of world history and of our personal histories, as well. He is Infinite and, from the perspective of the Infinite One, everything and everyone is equally significant.

If that is true then why doesn't He stop evil? Why doesn't He step in and prevent innocent suffering? The answer is because He has given us free will. Each of us has free choice to do good or evil. If He would stop me every time I wanted to hurt someone then I would not be exercising my free will but God's preprogrammed will. I would be a robot instead of a human being. My free will gives me my essential humanity, which is the foundation of life.

I strengthen my relationship with God when I exercise my free will to act in accordance with God's values and standards. If I do not follow God's will, then I am weakening my relationship with God. It is not a question of a red man with a pitchfork throwing lightning bolts at me. It is just that God becomes more distant from me. It is incredible to realize that it is actually *me* who determines how much of a relationship I have with God, and the quality and closeness of that relationship.

The alternative is to say that God created the world, and that it's running on its own, or that it just happened by accident. But that way of thinking is problematic, because if the world has no purpose, then neither do any of us!

Another problem I have with the "world has no purpose" scenario is that we see it is *not* true. The world seems to be directing itself toward a purpose, namely, morality. For example, our scientists are constantly developing new technologies to improve the quality of life and minimize human hardship. In economics, international organizations have formed to try to create unity and stability in the world economy. In politics, nations have banded together to rout out terrorism and destroy those who wish to perpetrate evil against civilization. If all of these areas on a macro level are geared toward a goal, then each life within the macro-system has a role to play, in some way, in furthering those goals. Thus, my life does have purpose. And so does yours.

30

WHAT'S THE POINT?

I HAVE OFTEN WONDERED why people put themselves in danger just for a thrill. Take bungee jumping, for example. This is the sport where you tie a rubber rope around your ankle and you jump off a bridge screaming "bungeeeee!" Just as you are about to hit the ground the rubber rope becomes taut and you are flung back up toward the top of the bridge from whence you came. You then bounce up and down until you come to a stop upside down, facing the ground.

I have one simple question. Why? The answer is that we have become so desensitized to the joy and thrill of everyday life that we need to put our lives at risk in order to just appreciate being alive. We only feel "alive" when we're on the edge. How can we appreciate being alive, without having to resort to bungee jumping?

A MYSTICAL PERSPECTIVE

KING SOLOMON, IN HIS BOOK *Koheles* (Ecclesiastes), explains to us why people go bungee jumping when he says, "Vanity of vanities; life is vanity." The Hebrew word for vanity is *hevel*, which means vapor. Life is vapor. And so are we. So we might as well "eat, drink, and bungee, for tomorrow we die."

The brilliant Talmudist and philosopher, Rabbi J. B. Soloveitchik, provides a unique comment on this verse. *Hevel*, he says, means that life is as precarious as vapor. One wrong turn to the left and it could be gone. He suggests that far from teaching us that life is meaningless and purposeless, King Solomon is teaching us that life is precious and must be appreciated. It must be cared for, nurtured and valued.

The proof that Rabbi Soloveitchik is correct about King Solomon's lesson to us is the second to last verse of the book of *Koheles*, which states:

"The conclusion of the matter, which summarizes everything, is: Fear God, and keep His commandments, for this is the whole duty of mankind."

If life is meaningless, then humanity can have no obligations or responsibilities. We should eat, drink and bungee till we drop. (Get it?) The fact that God commands us to perform mitzvot shows us that He believes that we can accomplish something worthwhile and significant with our lives.

We can take our situation, transform and develop it by comparing it to the standards and awe of the *Ein Sof*, and thereby become a little more Godlike than when we started. Every one of our actions can have cosmic significance.

31

GETTING MY ACT
TOGETHER

A SPIRITUAL PERSPECTIVE

WESTERN SOCIETY HAS A problem with the "G" word.
God. There, I said it. Modern people associate discussions about
God with "fundamentalism" and a "Middle Ages" mentality.
Few rational, 21st century people would consider discussions
about letting God into their lives as "politically correct."

"Too heavy, too religious," they would say. Psychologists
would say that humans have conjured up religion to calm our
psyche and to make sense of the pressures of life. They tell us that
we should rely only on progress, which is basically ourselves.

Recent studies have shown that most Americans, however,
do believe in God. In fact, most people in the world believe in
something "bigger than themselves". You can call it the "force."
We have called it the *Ein Sof*—the Infinite One.

Call it what you want, but that something is beyond me and you, and it is beyond this physical space we call the world. It is the source of spirituality. This spiritual force is the source of my soul—the source of everything. This force is the reason that there is good and bad in the world. It gives our lives a sense of destiny and purpose. It allows us to aspire to extraordinary things and to hope and to dream. All of these concepts and values are expressions of Godliness in the world. When I delve into my soul, I am yearning for a connection and a relationship with the Infinite—with my source.

It is high time we took our concept of God beyond the Sunday School conceptions of an old benevolent man with a flowing beard, white robes and sandals. Our perceptions in other areas of life, including career, relationships and goals have matured. So it is time for our conception of the Divine to mature as well.

"In the beginning God created the Heaven and the Earth" (Genesis 1:1). God brought the world into existence with a plan. And He placed Adam and Eve, which really means you and I, into the world to achieve our destiny and, through achieving our personal destiny, help the world achieve its purpose.

God does not need anything from you and me. He is quite perfect, thank you. He lacks nothing and needs nothing from me. He wants me, however, to act in a certain way, not for His benefit, but for my own benefit. Through bettering myself, and thereby bettering the world, I am acting as a partner with God in the actualization of His Plan for the Universe. He does not really need any "partners" but allows us to elevate ourselves by acting in "partnership" with Him.

While I was writing this paragraph, I received a letter in the mail with very disappointing news. I could have—and almost did—get into the down, negative mode of "Why is this happening to me?"

But I caught myself. "Calm down, take a deep breath and think. Access your spiritual center," I urged myself. "What can I do about this? What is a considered, mature approach to solving this problem?" You know something? It worked! I didn't solve the problem, but I came up with an alternative plan to deal with it. I went with the flow and I maintained an inner calm by willing myself to have "emotional stamina." That is truly bringing God into our lives. Then God meets us halfway and draws us even closer to Him, and to the truest most God-like version of ourselves.

A MYSTICAL PERSPECTIVE

WHENEVER MY KIDS BEGIN to demand my attention, I say to them, "Patience is a virtue." But sometimes too much patience is not good. Let me explain.

After the Jews endured two hundred and ten years of slavery and oppression in Egypt, the Torah states, "I have heard the Israelites cry...I will bring you out from the *sivlot* (burdens) of Egypt" (Exodus 6:6). One commentator, Rav Simcha Bunem of Pshyscha, explains the word *sivlot* to be connected to a similar word, *savlanut*, which means patience. When we read the verse again with this explanation, we find a profound message: "I have heard the Israelites' cry. I will bring you out of your patience with your burdens." The Israelites were no longer patient or accepting of their burdens, so they cried out to God and then He saved them.

The Israelites became "patient" with their lot in life. They regarded slavery as their natural state. They became accustomed to oppression; they bore their burdens too patiently. So God in effect said: When you are no longer accepting of your slavery, of your distance from me, and you become impatient with your burdens, then I will redeem you. God was waiting for the Israelites to desire and yearn for freedom. Once they were willing to change their attitude and to turn to God to take them out of Egypt, only then was God willing to redeem them.

There is a story told of a chicken farmer who once found some abandoned eggs in a field. He brought them to his farm and placed them together with some other eggs that a hen was sitting on and they hatched. They turned out to be eagles and not chickens. The eagles grew together with the other chicks and learned to act like chicks. They pecked at their food and walked, but they did not learn to fly. They became accustomed to their way of life. One day a hunter came to the chicken farm and noticed the eagles walking amongst the chickens. He went into the pen, picked up the eagles and brought them to the wild. "You are eagles, not chickens. You must learn to fly." The hunter taught them to fly, and one day they soared away and returned home to the wild.

When one is ready to "take control" of one's life and learns to become who one is supposed to be—then one will return home—to one's true self.

Until you're ready to take control, you may be stuck in the wrong pen. If you grow accustomed to living in the wrong pen, then you will certainly never achieve your potential.

The Torah tells us the manner in which God redeemed Israel from its patient acceptance of the burdens of Egypt as follows,

"And I will bear you on the wings of eagles and I will bring you to Me" (Exodus 19:4). When we are ready to get our act together, then we will turn to God and say, I am no longer patient with my negative mindset—I want to be redeemed! Then God will bear us on eagles' wings—and bring us to Him—and to a finer version of ourselves.

Did you enjoy this book?

Check out the *Judaism in a Nutshell* series...

Judaism in a Nutshell is a growing collection
of books by award-winning author Shimon Apisdorf
designed to make Judaism's most important ideas
and issues accessible to people who are
long on curiosity but short on time.

*"Apisdorf has the ability to communicate the practical wisdom of Judaism
and show how it relates to everyday life in the modern world."*
—The Jerusalem Report

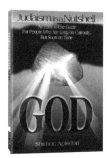

Judaism in a Nutshell: GOD

Brilliant rays of light guide the reader along a thought-provoking encounter with Judaism's ultimate insights into the reality of God. From philosophy, to history, to Kabbalah, this book covers the spectrum of the most profound of all topics.

Judaism in a Nutshell: HOLIDAYS

Holidays presents the major Jewish holidays in a broad, holistic framework. This book is able to transport readers with even the most minimal knowledge to an entirely new, often breath-taking level of understanding.

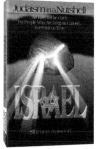

Judaism in a Nutshell: ISRAEL

For over three millenia, Israel has been a focal point for the Jews everywhere, and for the past century it has been on the center stage of world history. This book lucidly explains why Israel is so central to Judaism, how the modern State of Israel arose, and why Israel has fought so many wars with its neighbors and found peace to be so elusive.